MANPOWER PROGRAMS IN THE POLICY MIX

MANPOWER PROGRAMS IN THE POLICY MIX

Edited by
LLOYD ULMAN

The Johns Hopkins University Press

Baltimore and London

The Johns Hopkins University Press, Baltimore, Maryland 21218
The Johns Hopkins University Press Ltd., London

Library of Congress Catalog Card Number 72-11850
ISBN 0-8018-1452-9
Manufactured in the United States of America

Library of Congress Cataloging in Publication Data will be found on the last printed page of this book.

CONTENTS

NOTES ON CONTRIBUTORS

ROLF ANDERSSON is a Research Assistant at the Swedish Institute for Labor Studies, University of Stockholm.

R. A. GORDON is Professor of Economics at the University of California, Berkeley. His publications include *Business Leadership in the Large Corporation* (1945), *Business Fluctuations* (2nd ed., 1961), and *The Goal of Full Employment* (1967). He is also editor of *Toward a Manpower Policy* (1967) and co-author and co-editor of several volumes.

CHARLES C. HOLT is director of a research project on labor markets, inflation, and manpower policy at The Urban Institute, Washington, D.C. Previously he has done research at the University of Wisconsin, Carnegie Institute of Technology, and the London School of Economics, on economic stabilization, computer simulation, and production and employment planning. His publications include "Job Search, Phillips' Wage Relation, and Union Influence: Theory and Evidence," "Linear Decision Rules for Economic Stabilization and Growth," and *Planning Production, Inventories, and Work Force* (co-author, 1960).

SAR A. LEVITAN is Research Professor of Economics and Director of the Center for Manpower Policy Studies at The George Washington University. Among his most recent publications are *Human Resources and Labor Markets* (1972), which he co-authored, and *Blue-Collar Workers: A Symposium on Middle America* (1971) and *The Federal Social Dollar in Its Background* (1972), of which he is editor.

vii

C. DUNCAN MACRAE is manager of a research project on wage and related subsidies. Before joining The Urban Institute he was Assistant Professor of Economics at the Massachusetts Institute of Technology, where he was a consultant to the U.S. Department of Labor, the Urban League of Boston, and the Model Cities Program of Hoboken. His publications include "A Dual Maximum Principle for Discrete-Time Linear Systems with Economic Applications," "An Economic Evaluation of Urban Development," and "Economic Subsidies in the Urban Ghetto" (co-author).

RUDOLF MEIDNER, Director of the Swedish Institute for Labor Studies at the University of Stockholm from 1966 to 1971, is presently a staff member of Special Research Projects, Swedish Trade Union Confederation. He has published several articles on wage policy and unemployment and is co-author of *Fifteen Years of Wage Policy* (1972).

STUART O. SCHWEITZER is presently on the faculty of the School of Medicine, Georgetown University. He was on the research staff of The Urban Institute and prior to that was on the economics faculty at Wayne State University. His research and publications have been in the fields of labor economics, health, and human resources. His articles have appeared in *Industrial Labor Relations Review, Journal of Human Resources*, and *Brookings Papers on Economic Activity* (co-author), and he has presented papers before numerous professional meetings.

RALPH E. SMITH is on the research staff of The Urban Institute, Washington, D.C., where he has focused on modeling and estimating labor market relationships and evaluating the effects of manpower programs. His publications include "Apportionment of Funds under the Manpower Development Act of 1962," "A Job Search-Turnover Analysis of the Black-White Unemployment Ratio" (co-author), "The Dynamic Effect of Unemployment on Labor Force Participation" (co-author), and "The Opportunity Cost of Participating in a Training Program."

LESTER C. THUROW is Professor of Economics and Management at the Massachusetts Institute of Technology. His publications include *Investment in Human Capital* (1970) and *The Impact of Taxes on the American Economy* (1971).

LLOYD ULMAN, Professor of Economics and Director, Institute of Industrial Relations, University of California at Berkeley, is author of *The Rise of the National Trade Union* (2nd ed., 1966) and *The Government of the Steel Workers' Union* (1962), editor of *Challenges to Collective Bargaining* (1967), and co-author of *Wage Restraint: A Study of Incomes Policies in Western Europe* (1971).

MANPOWER PROGRAMS IN THE POLICY MIX

THE PROBLEMS IN POLICY CONTEXT

Lloyd Ulman

A public policy may invite criticism on the grounds that it is based on faulty diagnosis – that the problem to which it is addressed is not a problem (or *the* problem) at all. Or, if it is agreed that a policy target does exist, the policy in question might be faulted on the grounds that it cannot cope with the problem – that it is an ineffective instrument. To qualify as a potential recipient of criticism on both of these grounds, a policy must have addressed itself to more than one objective in the course of its existence. Contemporary manpower policy in the United States has, in the course of a decade of existence, established this qualification. It moved from an initial concern with technological unemployment and mature, experienced workers who were presumably the victims of the "new technology" to concentration on the young, the poor, and members of racial and ethnic minorities, many of whom have been victims of discrimination.

The policy's first critics argued that its early emphasis was misplaced since, contrary to the expectations of the "structuralists" and "Triple Revolution-aries," unemployment was reduced well below the Kennedy-Johnson "in-terim target" of 4 percent "with the use of simple fiscal and monetary pol-icies" (to quote a contributor to this volume). The policy's later orientation tapped new veins of criticism, although the limitations of simple fiscal and monetary policies became apparent as the latter provided a climate in which inflation increased as unemployment fell below 5 percent, while the structure of unemployment, in some dimensions, actually worsened. But some of the newer critics deny that manpower policy can be effective in reducing unemployment and raising the incomes of groups whose high unemployment results from social barriers. In somewhat related fashion, older critics, concentrating on cost-push behavior, which manifested itself most clearly in 1969-71 (after demand was restricted), deny that manpower policy can be effective in eliminating inflation which proceeds from social barriers — although the Swedish originators of the policy had made this claim on its behalf. And at times these later lines of criticism are supplemented by the suggestion that, since the private sector already invests rationally and heavily in the acquisition of labor market information and manpower development, the payoff to any appreciable public supplement is presumptively negligible (and conceivably negative).

Meanwhile, the policy has grown apace, as a bewildering variety of uncoordinated programs have sprung up. Levitan points out that federal outlays increased from less than a quarter-billion dollars in fiscal 1961 to over 3 billions in fiscal 1971. Thus the critics could argue that, when manpower policy was young and quantitatively insignificant, the alleged problem to which it was addressed seemed to go away without its help; after the policy reached an appreciable scale, its new targets would not yield to its approach. To which reply can be made — as it implicitly is by Holt, MacRae, Schweitzer, and Smith in this volume — that, for all its growth, the policy is not yet nearly big enough to be effective. It has certainly not reached the scale already achieved by the Swedes, as discussed in the essay by Meidner and Andersson. But it is big enough to be visible and for its future to be more widely discussed. This volume hopefully contributes to that discussion by presenting the views of several scholars on such macroeconomic and redistributional apsects of manpower policies as they have chosen to emphasize.

Their efforts contribute strong criticism of the policy's performance and careful discussion of its inherent limitations. But the contributors to this volume do not share the extreme pessimism of some of the critics; generally speaking, they favor active labor market policy as an instrument of redistribution or stabilization, or both. Holt and his associates and Gordon develop the complementary nature of these two objectives: if labor market measures can reduce the dispersion of unemployment rates, they can improve the inflation-unemployment trade-off; and, since the unemployment rates of disadvantaged minorities have been persistently high, manpower measures can also reduce racial and age-group differences in income. Gordon also dwells on a different aspect of the relationship between the two objectives: to the extent that labor market policies succeed in reducing sectoral dispersions in unemployment, they may also succeed "in making a given level of unemployment more acceptable." To Meidner and Andersson and Thurow, on the other hand, the two objectives appear more independent of each other. Thurow doubts that manpower policy could effect such redistributions as

Gordon contemplates, except under conditions of very low unemployment and inflation; however, he is quite willing to accept inflation if it is associated with full employment and egalitarian redistribution of income. But these two positions might be less opposed than they appear to be. If the effect of reducing the dispersion of unemployment around a given level of unemployment is sufficiently adverse to enough people, unemployment might become less, rather than more, acceptable politically, and inflation might become less unpalatable.

Meidner and Andersson, in the Swedish tradition, are concerned with the impacts, potential and actual, of active labor market policy on price behavior. But they are also willing to employ the policy as a redistributive instrument in the sense of Gordon and Holt and, indeed, to the point "that satisfies the wishes of the citizens as regards employment (whether or not they are in the labor force and whether or not their marginal productive input corresponds to the market wage)." In holding that it might be desirable to employ manpower development programs even where the costs incurred might exceed the economic benefits, Thurow makes much the same point, as does Levitan (and the Council of Economic Advisers in 1967).[1]

Whether or not they might differ in the extent to which they would be willing to deploy active labor market policies, the authors agree that the existence of market imperfections constitutes a basis for the case in favor of these policies. Since this ranges them against the laissez-faire (or who needs it?) line of criticism, a few comments on how some imperfections might in principle be countered by public programs of manpower development may be in order.

In the first place, to the extent that individuals must incur the costs of their own training — especially when the skills to be acquired would make them more valuable to other employers as well as to their own — there is a case for subsidizing the training of poorer individuals, particularly those who are likely targets of discrimination. Such individuals, as Thurow points out, are apt to have exceptionally high rates of time preference precisely because they are poor — the marginal utility to them of a dollar in wages foregone during the training period is exceptionally high — and because their opportunities are limited — the private return on a training investment is likely to be exceptionally low. Moreover, there can be little doubt that any would-be borrower for whom discrimination had made the labor market imperfect would find himself regarded as an exceptionally poor risk by any potential lender in the capital market. Subsidies, even if provided on a scale sufficient to eliminate or overcompensate for the direct and indirect costs of training, cannot by themselves overcome the obstacles to career development thrown

---

[1] U.S., *Economic Report of the President*, January 1967, p. 108.

up by poverty and discrimination, but they would in principle have a useful role to perform in helping to neutralize these disadvantages.

Other types of imperfection, originating on both the buyers' and the sellers' side of the labor market, also create a case on equitable grounds for the provision of active labor market programs. Oddly enough, they may do so by generating excessive "credentialism" — i.e., demand for, and supply of, labor whose degree of formal schooling is in excess of the requirements of a perfectly competitive labor market. In a forthcoming paper, V. L. Rawlins and I suggest that this can result when employers pay wages above market-clearing levels.[2] They may do so by design, as in the case of the large, "monopsonistic" employer who seeks the capability of screening job applicants for "quality." Or they may do so out of compulsion, as in the case of the unionized employer who seeks to absorb part of the increased labor costs resulting from collective bargaining by hiring some labor of presumably higher quality. (A nonunion employer who maintains a union-preventive wage would make the same adjustment.) In either case the employer must incur selection costs. Moreover, to the extent that his employees' wages are raised above their "transfer earnings" and that their quit rates are consequently reduced, he finds it profitable to pay for training of a more "general," as well as of a more "specific," nature. Hence he finds that by hiring workers with more impressive educational credentials he can minimize screening costs and, hopefully, training costs as well. Such processes tend to force workers with lower educational credentials into lower-paying and otherwise less attractive labor markets. Thus the educational gains registered by Negroes and other nonwhites in the postwar period might have been robbed of a considerable degree of economic payoff. It is understandable that the nonwhite should find conspiracy where others might deduce only the workings of the modern marketplace. Under the circumstances, and given the fact that formal educational inequalities still exist, some compensatory training — and compensatory credentialing — might be in order.

Still another class of labor market imperfections, manifested in the existence of shortages (or bottlenecks) in specific skilled occupations, can be generated and renewed by cyclical alternation and by growth of demand. The work of Sara Behman, Holt, Schultze, and others establishes the inflationary influence of skill shortages during periods of expansion.[3] But why should

[2] V. Lane Rawlins and Lloyd Ulman, "The Utilization of College Trained Manpower in the United States," in *Higher Education and the Labor Market*, to be published by the Carnegie Commission on Higher Education.

[3] Sara Behman, "Wage-Determination Process in U.S. Manufacturing," *Quarterly Journal of Economics*, February 1968, pp. 117–42; Charles L. Schutze, "Has the Phillips Curve Shifted? Some Additional Evidence," *Brookings Papers on Economic Activity*, 2 (1971): 452–68.

such apparently serious shortages occur during an upswing, given the exist-ence of excess supplies of skilled (as well as other) workers during the preced-ing recession? The answer, I believe, is that it is precisely during the slack period, when there is unemployment and underutilization of skilled labor, that potential, or full employment, shortages begin to build up. This happens because normal withdrawals from the skilled work forces (e.g., withdrawls due to death and retirement, but not to discouragement caused by cyclical unemployment) are not wholly replaced. Nor is provision made for increased demand, which is generated in the course of secular economic growth and realized during upswings in activity. There is little incentive to invest in human as well as physical capital when demand is generally slack; and there is consequently a bunching of investment in training during the upswing, as stockpiles of downgraded skilled workers and supplies of available rehires begin to dry up. To be sure, supplies in many categories can be replenished by company training, promotion, and increased hiring at low entry levels. In the case of skills recruited directly from the outside, however, firms bid up wages in the marketplace as the incidence of quits rises among groups with lateral (interemployer) instead of vertical mobility. Higher wages and more vacancies induce more investment in training, but training takes time. Skill shortages thus tend to appear and persist when the economy is still quite short of full employment. To this extent, there is a case for training subsidies during periods of slack activity.

The contributors to this volume, however, are less concerned with the causes of imperfections than with their effects and with evidence of their growth. Both Gordon and Holt, building on their earlier work, establish that the inflationary potential of the economy is an increasing function of the dispersion of sectoral unemployment rates (weighted by labor force or by employment). They find no evidence of increasing occupational dispersion and hence, in this respect, no sign of adverse structural changes induced by changes in the composition of demand for labor. This might be taken as lack of support for one version of the skill-twist hypothesis; and Holt and his associates' finding of diminishing geographical dispersion of unemployment is further grist for the skeptics' mill.

On the other hand, this volume presents fresh evidence to support Gor-don's long-standing conclusion that "the most serious problems of structural unemployment . . . since the mid-fifties have arisen from changes on the sup-ply side of the labor market rather than on the demand side." Unemployment dispersion by age and sex increased dramatically with the disproportionate growth of teenagers and women in the labor force and with the dispropor-tionate rise in their unemployment rates. Associated with these changes has been a marked decline in the share of the labor force accounted for by men of prime working age and a marked decrease in their unemployment rates ment as an explanatory variable in a wage-change equation, Holt and his associates, like George Perry,[4] regard the recorded increase in this dispersion as a major inflationary influence. And, looking ahead, Gordon finds little prospect for self-correction. The work force will have a larger proportion of young men out of their teens, but the proportion of prime-age males — whose unemployment rates have already sunk to bottleneck levels — will continue to shrink. Moreover, the shares of high-unemployment groups — women and nonwhites — will increase.

Although the worsening trade-off between unemployment and inflation can thus be associated with changes originating on the supply side of the labor market, bottlenecks could have developed only if employers had been unable or unwilling to substitute labor which had become more plentiful for labor which had become less plentiful. Unwillingness of workers in the former category to apply for jobs of the type performed by workers in short supply could not have played much of a role in producing bottlenecks, in view of the relatively increased rates of unemployment among younger people and women. Employers, on the other hand, might have found it preferable to bid for the services of men in their thirties and forties if they felt that workers in the more plentiful categories had less education or training and were less capable on that account. Gordon's finding of a relatively great decline in labor force participation among the poorly educated is consistent with this hypothesis. This finding also helps to account for the fact that, while there has been a recent decline in the dispersion of unemployment by color, it has been matched, according to Gordon, by a relative and absolute decline in participation rates for nonwhite males over the age of twenty-five. The latter are less well educated than whites in the same age group.

Another of Gordon's findings — that an increased proportion of the unemployed was accounted for by those without previous work experience — is also consistent with the hypothesis that the more abundant sources of labor supply were imperfect substitutes for the scarcer varieties because they had received less training. On the other hand, the young were, by historical standards, very well endowed with formal education; and this should tend to reduce the length and cost of on-the-job training for them. In fact, high unemployment rates among the young and the inexperienced suggests another possible explanation of the inflationary increase in the demographic dispersions of unemployment: rigidity in industrial and occupational wage structures. This hypothesis holds that wage structures have not been sufficiently flexible to make it profitable enough for employers to hire and train less experienced and/or less educated people rather than bid up the wages of

[4]George L. Perry, "Changing Labor Markets and Inflation," *Brookings Papers on Economic Activity*, 1970, no. 3, pp. 411–41.

experienced workers. Under rigid wage structures, it would have been profitable to absorb the former in the increased proportions in which they came onto the market only if changes in technology and/or in the composition of demand indicated substitution in favor of less experienced, less trained, or less educated labor. Such changes, had they occurred, would have been opposite to those postulated by the proponents of the skill-twist hypothesis. However, some of the same adverse effects attributed by this hypothesis to a relative decrease in demand for untrained labor could have been produced by a relative increase in the supply of such labor, taken in conjunction with an unchanged composition of demand and sufficiently rigid wage structures.

Of course, while many market imperfections are attributable to institutions such as collective bargaining and minimum wages, to imitative wage-setting policies of employers, and to social discrimination, others in a sense result from changes in conditions of demand or supply, which require time for adjustment. Moreover, the adverse impact of labor market imperfections, whatever their origin, varies with the magnitude of such changes. Nevertheless, dealing explicitly with the role of wage structures might help to make more understandable one distinctive characteristic of recent unemployment. In contrast to unemployment characterized by long duration of joblessness — the type of "structural unemployment" which might be expected to result from massive technological displacement of a group of experienced workers — unemployment in the sixties has been characterized by relatively short duration and relatively high incidence and turnover, especially when the overall rate of unemployment has been relatively low. Unemployment characterized by high rates of turnover has usually been described as "frictional"; and, since it results from frequent quitting as well as layoffs, it is often regarded as "voluntary" as well. Hence Thurow argues that manpower policy ought not be directed toward reducing the minimum achievable rate of overall unemployment, since "no one is worried about voluntary unemployment at a 3 percent level of general unemployment." But what about sectors of the labor force where high-turnover unemployment greatly exceeds the average level and where it is frequently associated with low rates of labor force participation as well?

It has been argued that for some such groups unemployment, at least in part, might still be regarded as voluntary, since, at prevailing wages, members of the "secondary" work force may have preferable nonmarket alternatives at home or in school.[5] The latter might thus be contrasted with persons who would be willing to take a job in their line of work at the going wage — or

[5] Jacob Mincer, "Labor-Force Participation and Unemployment: A Review of Recent Evidence," in *Prosperity and Unemployment*, ed. R. A. Gordon and Margaret S. Gordon (New York: John Wiley & Sons, 1966), pp. 101–2.

even at a lower wage — if they could find such work. But, for many people in high-turnover groups, wages are "too low" because their nonmarket alternatives are clearly detrimental to social welfare and destructive of individual self-regard and happiness. Wages are too low for them relative to wages in entry-level jobs which are not available to them; they seem to be locked into "secondary" labor markets;[6] and they tend frequently to quit — jobs, labor force, and school — out of frustration and resentment at their segregation. Segregation is caused in part by direct discrimination and sometimes by direct restriction of entry; but restriction of entry into protected labor markets can result simply from the maintenance of high wages in them. (Hence the old craft disclaimer: "We don't discriminate on the basis of color; we discriminate against *everyone*.") The inverse correlation between industry wage rates and quit rates strongly suggests that wage-structure rigidities contribute to lack of opportunity and "pathological instability" (the phrase is Hall's) in unprotected labor markets.[7] People do not quit good, high-wage jobs as frequently as they quit low-wage, dead-end jobs, nor do they quit them for the same reasons. It is interesting to note that Gordon distinguishes between "differentially high frictional unemployment which is offset by relatively high wages or other attractions of the job" and that which is not so offset — and that he classifies the latter as "structural" unemployment.

Indeed, active labor market policy can be defined and distinguished from certain other policies with respect to labor market imperfections and wage rigidites. We have already considered two types of "high-wage" markets: those in which wages are pulled up by shortages of highly trained labor and those in which wages are pushed up by institutional or conventional forces and where shortages are not prevalent. (In the former, supply is highly inelastic; in the latter, it is highly elastic at the going wage.) We have also considered certain groups of unemployed and underemployed persons who may be said to be excluded from the first type of market by lack of education and training and from the second by lack of job openings for which they would — or easily could — be qualified. The latter in principle might be absorbed into more desirable markets in one (or more) of the following ways:

[6]P. B. Doeringer and M. J. Piore, *Internal Labor Markets and Manpower Analysis* (Indianapolis: D. C. Heath & Co., 1971).

[7]See L. Ulman, "Labor Mobility and the Industrial Wage Structure in the Postwar United States," *Quarterly Journal of Economics*, February 1965, pp. 73–97. This association holds even after allowance is made for differences in skill content, which reflect differences in training investments. See Mark A. Lutz, "The Equilibrium Industrial Wage Structure," Ph.D. diss., University of California, Berkeley. Consistent with the foregoing is the finding by Wachter of "premiums" on the wages of skilled, high-wage labor. See M. L. Wachter, "Cyclical Variation in the Interindustry Wage Structure," *American Economic Review*, March 1970, pp. 75–84.

1. Structural change, which would induce greater flexibility in relative wages and thus more employment in the second type of market, where wages are set by collective bargaining or discretionary management "policy." If some of the shortages in markets of the first variety are caused by institutional (including legal) barriers to entry, and if structural reforms eliminated such shortages, employment in the first type of market also would be increased.

2. An increase in overall demand, which would also increase employment in the "institutionalized" markets, but which would concomitantly raise demand and thus contribute further to wage increases in both sectors (causing the economy to move up along a Phillips curve).

3. An increase in overall demand, as above, but one accompanied by an incomes policy, which would permit demand to increase in the institutionalized markets but which would hold down the rate of wage increase in those markets (thereby shifting the Phillips curve to the left and downward).

4a. An active labor market, or manpower, policy which would simultaneously reduce unemployment and the rate of wage increase by reducing excess supplies of labor and increasing supplies of qualified labor in shortage categories. This would shift the Phillips curve downward by shifting the sectoral supply curves in opposite directions rather than by altering relative wages (as is contemplated under both structural reform and incomes policy). It would operate primarily by increasing employment in the excess demand sector rather than in the excess supply sector. As the Holt paper indicates, this set of policies could be designed to improve labor mobility by increasing the efficiency of employment agencies and counseling services as well as by manpower training.

4b. An active labor market policy which would operate by increasing demand selectively — as by concentrating reflation in labor-surplus areas, in the manner described graphically by Meidner and Andersson. Such a policy would be designed primarily to cope with geographic "compartmentalization"; but it could be employed in conjunction with policies described under (4a), as indeed it has been in the United States and elsewhere, and as Meidner and Andersson insist it should be.

In fact, selective job creation in the public service may be employed on a significant scale in this country and not solely as a rather temporary, contracyclical device. Manpower training is presumably of only limited effectiveness where the problem is more lack of motivation, induced by low wages and deadend jobs, than lack of capacity. Neither might selective (relative) reduction in the minimum wage — which is the form of structural change most commonly advocated as a cure for certain types of structural unemployment — be effective in coping with "voluntary" unemployment traceable in part to wages that are too low rather than too high. Thus public service employment can be regarded as a branch of manpower policy which at least potentially might prove a superior substitute for certain types of structural reform and as both substitute for, and complement to, other types of manpower policy.

Thus manpower policy can be viewed as an alternative to structural change in the labor market, to general reflationary measures, or to incomes policy. In Sweden, as Meidner and Andersson explain, it has been regarded as an alternative to all three. It was originated there by Gösta Rehn and Rudolf Meidner, who were then economists with the Swedish Federation of Labor, because, given the country's very ambitious unemployment goals, incomes policy was ineffective in preventing wage drift and also because wage drift frustrated the labor movement's attempts to implement a "solidaristic" (or egalitarian) wage policy. The task of active labor market policy was to introduce reflation by selective measures aimed simultaneously at pockets of unemployment and at labor bottlenecks. This was supposed to reduce the level of aggregate demand required to maintain any given level of employment and, consequently, to reduce the ability of both employers and union groups to generate wage drift. The Swedes have taken their innovation seriously, judging from the documentation of its growth in expenditure and coverage (to over 4 percent of the labor force) presented by Meidner and Andersson. They conclude significantly that "Keynesian fiscal policy has become less significant in Sweden."

But manpower policy can be regarded as an alternative to the other policies only to the extent that it is effective in practice. The contributors to this volume, while advocating the use of manpower policies in one role or another, are under no illusions on this score. Levitan's paper subjects many of the programs to strenuous (although sympathetic) criticism. He observes that, despite greatly increased budgets, the number of nonagricultural placements made by public employment services actually declined in the sixties. He makes it clear that training subsidies to employers may have fallen under the curse of their class to the extent that the training would have been provided in the absence of public financial support — and that proposed tax incentives would suffer the same fate. Moreover, some of the training and income maintenance provided directly to the trainee seems to have provided more income maintenance than training. In view of experience to date, Levitan is not sanguine about the economic prospects of plans to endow significant numbers of welfare recipients with marketable levels of productivity.

While Gordon credits some of the manpower policies with helping to increase the representation of Negroes in some occupations, he assigns them no credit in the narrowing of the dispersion of occupational unemployment rates, "most of which occurred before present manpower programs had had the time to become very effective." Thurow questions the policies' effectiveness in coping with unemployment due to "bad habits and low work standards," which have to be corrected by "socialization" and "industrial discipline." And he, together with the other American contributors, advocate more emphasis on "creaming," or training those already employed to fill skill shortages and thus to vacate lower-skilled jobs, which the inexperienced and the unemployed might then be trained for more efficiently. It is also noted that, while increased enrollment in manpower programs has tended to reduce unemployment, this could also generate some inflationary effect by removing people from the work force. (Thus the programs would simply be moving the economy up an existing Phillips curve rather than shifting the curve downward.) On the other hand, to the extent that labor market policies make information about job openings and worker availability easier and cheaper to come by, they might increase turnover and thus tend to increase unemployment, as Gordon observes.

Moreover, while the idea of a contracyclical labor market policy (the so-called manpower trigger) is attractive in principle, its effectiveness, as the policy grows in magnitude, depends increasingly on the efficiency of economic planning and, in particular, on the ability to forecast changes in the pattern of labor demand. Finally, labor market policies have not been able to prevent perverse shifts in inflation-unemployment trade-offs in either the United States (as noted by Gordon) or Sweden. In the United States this could be taken as evidence of the need for a more ambitious use of the policy; this is essentially the position taken by Holt, MacRae, Schweitzer, and Smith. In Sweden, however, where the policy has already grown to considerable size, this explanation would be much less convincing. Meidner and Andersson rather tentatively attribute a worsening in the Swedish trade-off to increased industrial concentration caused by the increasing scope of foreign competition. But they also reach the very interesting conclusion that the policy has been employed asymmetrically. "It has proven easier – politically – to use selective assistance as an alternative to general measures to maintain purchasing power during downswings than actively to subdue excess demand during booms."

Indeed, the adverse trade-off experience of Sweden, and of other Western countries as well, suggests that the somewhat distinctive demographic developments in the United States in the 1960s might not have exerted as unique an inflationary effect as they are credited with. And, if cost-push influences also played a significant inflationary role, how effective could one have expected labor market policies to be?

Yet these policies cannot be dismissed as ineffective, either here or abroad. The numerous benefit-cost studies of specific programs which have been made are subject to methodological difficulties – notably, the difficulty of securing sufficiently comparable "control groups" and of failing to allow for the displacement of qualified workers who did not undergo training in the program in question. On the other hand, the favorable results have been too pronounced and widespread (in Sweden as well as in the United States) to be dismissed by the policymaker. Moreover, some studies suggest that certain American programs might indeed have been effective in improving the work habits and outlooks of disadvantaged younger persons; and Meidner and Andersson report success in the post-training placement of unemployed or hard-to-place persons under Swedish programs. As far as the inflationary effect of withdrawing trainees from the labor market is concerned, Gordon concludes that it could not have been great in the case of teenagers and other "secondary" workers, whose unemployment rates were already at high levels. And the danger of graduate trainees "bumping" or displacing experienced workers could be minimized, according to Thurow, by concentrating training during upswings rather than during downswings, and by directing it toward observed vacancies.

Given a mixed bag of evidence on the performance and apparent potentialities of manpower policy, the policymaker might well look upon it more as a supplement to, than as a substitute for, alternative policies. But, given the limited effectiveness of the alternatives, manpower policy can be a valuable supplement. Thus, since it is axiomatic that the value of training depends on the availability of jobs for the qualified trainees, a suitably expansive aggregate-demand policy is required. For the same reason, as Thurow and Gordon insist, an effective antidiscrimination policy also is a necessary complement to manpower development programs. However, the latter may be required to give effect to expansionary-demand management, on the one hand, and to antidiscrimination policies, on the other. Manpower development could help to implement antidiscrimination policies by furnishing an effective reply to the protest that "we would take more of them in if we could find qualified ones." Indeed, the existence of trained members of underprivileged minorities can exert a salutary coercive effect on employers and unions, for it represents a potential competitive threat. In this sense, therefore, the provision of training can help to create some of the vacancies for which the training is provided. The strength of such a competitive threat should not be exaggerated, but, in view of the difficulties involved in enforcing antidiscrimination policies in the face of limited economic opportunity, even a modest aid to enforcement should be regarded seriously.

Can the relationship between active labor market policy and incomes policy be regarded as complementary? The former, as noted above, originated as an alternative to the latter, and proponents of the two approaches have tended to regard one another as natural enemies ever since. Perhaps this relationship reflects the rivalry between those two socially pioneering countries, Sweden and the Netherlands (the birthplace of modern incomes policy).

Perhaps it reflects the difference in outlook between the Department of Labor and the Council of Economic Advisers here at home. Perhaps people who are concerned with vertical supply curves resent the concern of others with horizontal supply curves, and vice versa. In the United States, opposition to incomes policy is contributed by (but not restricted to) those who deny the existence of cost-push influences, but, in Sweden, proponents of labor market policy argued that it was a superior instrument for dealing with cost-push. In any event — and whatever their respective merits and drawbacks on other grounds — the two approaches ought not be regarded as mutually exclusive. Not only do organizational influences coexist with other sources of labor market imperfection but interaction occurs. Unionism can help to cause shortages in some sectors. It might also help to spread shortage-generated wage increases to occupations and industries where labor is in excess supply. Thus, the more effective either policy becomes in its own domain, the more effective it helps to make the other. What helps to clean the pot helps to clean the kettle.

CHAPTER ONE

SOME MACROECONOMIC ASPECTS OF MANPOWER POLICY

R. A. Gordon

Increasing attention has been paid in recent years to the possible contributions that manpower policy can make to the achievement of the standard macroeconomic goals.[1] It is to this issue that the present essay is addressed. In particular, to what extent can manpower programs contribute to a better reconciliation of the conflicting goals of full employment and price stability than the United States has in fact achieved in recent years? In dealing with this question, I shall pay particular attention to the composition of unemployment as it is affected by the changing patterns of demand for, and supply of, labor.

MANPOWER POLICY AND THE PHILLIPS CURVE

There is no need to review here the burgeoning literature, theoretical and empirical, on the Phillips curve. The evidence strongly points to the fact that there *is* a trade-off between unemployment and the rate of wage inflation — or, as Charles Holt puts it, "that the Phillips relation is an important characteristic of labor markets in many economies, our own included."[2] We

---

[1] I should like to thank Dennis Roth for his help in the preparation of this essay. I should also like to acknowledge the assistance provided by the Institute of Industrial Relations at the University of California, Berkeley, and by the National Manpower Policy Task Force, Washington, D.C.

[2] Charles C. Holt, "How Can the Phillips Curve be Moved to Reduce Both Inflation and Unemployment," in Edmund S. Phelps *et al., Microeconomic Foundations of Employment and Inflation Theory* (New York: Norton, 1970), p. 253. References to some of the recent empirical literature will be found in subsequent footnotes.

can distinguish between a short-run and a long-run relation between the rate of change in wages and the level of unemployment, the latter relation being more stable than the former.[3]

The conclusion that appropriately designed manpower programs can improve the trade-off between inflation and unemployment rests on the belief that such programs can shift the long-run Phillips curve to the left. It is less widely recognized that some ways of shifting the Phillips curve to the left can lead to a "tangency solution" that makes a given level of *total* unemployment more acceptable than it was before. This point may deserve brief elaboration.

Figure 1-1 presents the familiar diagram which illustrates a "tangency solution."[4] The curve XX' is derived from the Phillips curve;[5] UU' reflects the policymaker's preference function for different combinations of total unemployment and rate of change in prices. Assume that manpower policy does succeed in shifting the inflation-unemployment curve leftward from XX' to YY'. With unchanged preferences as to the marginal rate of substitution between the rate of price change and the level of unemployment, the tangency solution will be at B, yielding both a lower rate of price increase (OP_2) and less unemployment (OU_2) than before.

Now assume what is certainly true, that the policymaker's conception of economic welfare depends not only on the rate of inflation and the total

[3] The short-run Phillips curve seems to shift frequently both because other variables, in addition to the unemployment rate, also affect wages and because the relation between the rate of change in wages, on the one hand, and unemployment and other variables, on the other hand, is a dynamic one, involving lags. Thus the same unemployment rate at different times may result in different rates of wage increase depending on the values of the unemployment rate and other variables in the recent past. The "long-run" Phillips curve represents the relation between the change in wages and the unemployment rate when all explanatory variables remain unchanged for a period long enough for all lagged effects to make themselves felt. We shall return to this distinction in a later section. For a useful discussion, see Charles C. Holt *et al.*, *The Unemployment-Inflation Dilemma: A Manpower Solution* (Washington, D.C.: The Urban Institute, 1971), chap. 1.

[4] See R. G. Lipsey, "Structural and Deficient-Demand Unemployment Reconsidered," in *Employment Policy and the Labor Market*, ed. A. M. Ross (Berkeley and Los Angeles: University of California Press, 1965), p. 211.

[5] Strictly speaking, the Phillips curve relates the change in *wages* to the rate of unemployment. By positing a relation between price changes and wage changes, we can also relate the rate of change in prices to unemployment. To speak of a trade-off between unemployment and inflation (i.e., the rate of change in *prices*), we need a minimum of two functional relationships: one between wage change, on the one hand, and unemployment, current and past price changes, and other relevant variables, on the other; and a second relation between the change in prices and the variables which presumably explain the behavior of prices (including wages, as, for example, reflected in unit labor costs). And, of course, if we want to explain the behavior of most or all of the other explanatory variables that help to explain the behavior of wages and prices, we need as many equations as there are endogenous variables to be explained. For an example of an attempt to explain both wage and price changes, see the papers by Robert J. Gordon in *Brookings Papers on Economic Activity*, 1970, no. 1, and 1971, no. 1.

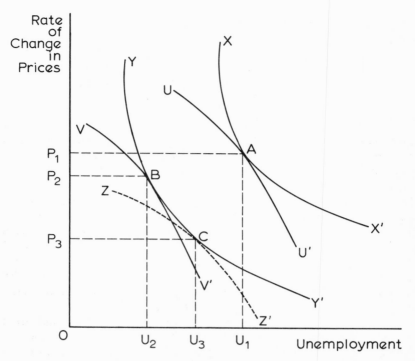

Figure 1-1. The Trade-Off between Inflation and Unemployment

unemployment rate but also on the dispersion of unemployment rates in different sectors of the labor force when the latter is classified in particular ways — say, by race, sex, and age. We can restate this algebraically as

$$Z = f(\dot{P}, u, u_1, u_2, \ldots u_n).$$

That is to say, welfare (Z) depends not only on the rate of change in prices ($\dot{P}$) and overall unemployment (u) but also on the unemployment rates of particular groups ($u_1, u_2, \ldots u_n$).[6] If, for example, new manpower programs not only shift the Phillips curve to the left but also significantly reduce the high unemployment rates of particular groups (for example, blacks and teenagers), the policymaker's indifference curve may shift from VV' in Figure 1-1 to ZZ', yielding an unemployment-inflation trade-off of only OP_3 for the rate of price increase and as much as OU_3 in unemployment. Here man-

[6]See R. A. Gordon, *The Goal of Full Employment* (New York: Wiley, 1967), pp. 165–66.

power policy has reduced the rate of inflation both by shifting the Phillips curve and by making a given level of total unemployment more acceptable.[7]

ANOTHER LOOK AT THE NATURE OF FRICTIONAL AND STRUCTURAL UNEMPLOYMENT

The Phillips curve reflects the response of wages to different relations between demand and supply in the national labor market, given the set of conditions that determine the position and shape of the curve. The relation between demand and supply in the labor market can be reasonably approximated by comparing unemployment with job vacancies. Indeed, some writers have sought to define a situation of full employment as one in which the total number of job vacancies equals the level of unemployment, and have implied at the same time that such a relationship would not lead to an increase in money wages or would lead to no more of an increase than could be absorbed by the growth of manhour productivity. This is an unjustified inference.[8] Nonetheless, the relation between vacancies and unemployment provides a good starting point for considering how and to what extent manpower policy can shift the Phillips curve to the left.[9] The next few paragraphs lean heavily on the work of Charles C. Holt and his colleagues.[10]

In the last few years, a number of economists have developed variants of the "search theory" of employment, unemployment, and wages.[11] Some of these variants assume a homogeneous labor market, in which all workers are equally qualified for all jobs. Where this assumption is made, the level of total vacancies and the level of unemployment, when both are equal to each other, depend on what is generally, if loosely, referred to as frictional unemployment. The Phillips curve can be shifted to the left by reducing the amount of

---

[7]This same point was made by Lloyd Ulman in 1967 at the Ulricehamn conference on incomes policy, held in honor of Erik Lundberg, and is repeated in Lloyd Ulman and Robert J. Flanagan, *Wage Restraint: A Study of Incomes Policies in Western Europe* (Berkeley and Los Angeles: University of California Press, 1971), p. 247.

[8]See Holt, "How Can the Phillips Curve be Moved to Reduce Both Inflation and Unemployment?" p. 241; and R. A. Gordon, *The Goal of Full Employment*, p. 74.

[9]A number of writers have formally derived the Phillips curve relation from the relationship between vacancies and unemployment. See, for example, the previously cited paper by Holt and the references there to his earlier work; Holt *et al., The Unemployment-Inflation Dilemma*; Bent Hansen, "Excess Demand, Unemployment, Vacancies, and Wages," *Quarterly Journal of Economics*, 84 (February 1970): 1–23.

[10]See particularly Holt, "How Can the Phillips Curve be Moved to Reduce Both Inflation and Unemployment?" For the purposes of the present essay, a particular advantage of Holt's work is that, unlike a number of other contributors to the literature on a "search theory" of labor markets, Holt explicitly takes account of the fact that the national labor market is segmented.

[11]See particularly the papers in Phelps *et al., Microeconomic Foundations of Employment and Inflation Theory.*

frictional unemployment. The latter, in turn, depends upon the frequency with which workers enter the state of unemployment (from layoffs, quits, and entry into the labor force) and the average time spent in search before a new job is found.

Holt's version of this approach takes account of segmentation of the labor force and the fact that the relation between unemployment and vacancies may be different in different labor submarkets. Put very briefly and perhaps too simply, his analysis suggests that the position and shape of the Phillips curve depends on the turnover rate, mean search time, the probability that a job interview will result in placement, the size of the labor force, the number of sectors into which the labor force is segmented, and the extent to which the ratio of vacancies to unemployment differs in the different segments of the labor market. The more the labor force is segmented and the wider the dispersion of the vacancy-unemployment ratio is among the different segments, the greater will be the rise in wages for any given rate of total unemployment.[12]

This formulation can be translated into the less precise statement that the position of the Phillips curve depends upon the amount of frictional and structural unemployment. The rate of turnover of jobs and the average time involved in searching for a new job (at a full-employment level of aggregate demand) determine frictional (including seasonal) unemployment. In Holt's analysis, the segmentation of labor markets increases the amount of frictional unemployment, even if the ratio of vacancies to unemployment is the same in all sectors. This is because of economies of scale in the search process. The larger the labor market, the lower need be the percentage rates of unemployment and vacancies in order to achieve a given flow of new hires, assuming the period typically spent searching for a new job.

Persistent differences in vacancy-unemployment ratios in different labor submarkets point to the existence of a type of unemployment which can be called "structural." The notion of "structural unemployment" has always given economists trouble – but never more so than in the debate over the relative roles of deficient aggregate demand and "structural" factors in creating the relatively high unemployment rates of the early 1960s. The recent tendency has been to play down the difference between structural and frictional unemployment. Instead, emphasis is placed on the high rates of labor turnover, in which case the duration of unemployment is not necessarily very long, even in labor markets with unemployment rates considerably above the national rate. Relatively high unemployment among teenagers, for example, reflects not so much prolonged periods of unemployment for this group as

[12] See Holt, "How Can the Phillips Curve Be Moved to Reduce Both Inflation and Unemployment?" pp. 236–41; and Holt *et al., The Unemployment-Inflation Dilemma,* pp. 52ff.

relatively high turnover rates.[13] Turnover rates would be higher and search time perhaps longer for blacks than for whites in the same age-sex groups.[14] In these terms, what was once referred to as structural unemployment becomes differentially high frictional unemployment.[15]

For reasons which (I hope) are more than merely a matter of personal taste, I am reluctant to see the notion of structural unemployment merged into the concept of (differentially high) frictional unemployment. Frictional unemployment in the conventional sense is relatively high among prime-age white males in the construction trades — both because of seasonal changes in employment opportunities and because of the need for frequent shifting among jobs. But certainly it both stretches the meaning of a widely (if loosely) used notion and gives a misleading impression as to causes to refer to some part of the above average unemployment rate in these generally highly paid trades with restricted entry as "structural" unemployment.

In the last few years, the unemployment rate (seasonally adjusted) in the construction industry has ranged, very roughly, between 1½ and 2 times the national rate. More or less the same relation has existed between the rate for nonfarm laborers and the national rate. The rate for nonwhites has been nearly twice the national rate. We can say that all three of these relatively high unemployment rates resulted from abnormally high job turnover, which was perhaps connected with longer-than-average search in the third case and probably so in the second case. In this sense, "frictional" unemployment is higher than the national average for all three groups. But I think there is a sense in which the nonwhites and the unskilled laborers suffer from "structural" unemployment and the (at least skilled) construction workers do not. Relatively high unemployment in the construction industry in prosperous times results from the technical characteristics of the industry and affects workers who have considerable mobility — i.e., have the ability to move into

[13] The average duration of unemployment for youth is actually significantly less than that for adults. See, for example, U.S., Department of Labor, *Manpower Report of the President*, April 1971, Table A-20, pp. 227–28.

[14] The contrast between the relative importance of long-term unemployment among white and nonwhite unemployed workers has declined significantly in the last few years. See *ibid.*

[15] See, for example, Robert E. Hall, "Why Is the Unemployment Rate So High at Full Employment?" *Brookings Papers on Economic Activity*, 1970, no. 3, pp. 369–402. See also the comments by Charles Holt, *ibid.* pp. 405–8, particularly his statement that "the search theory now ought to be characterized as a search-turnover theory." Hall makes a distinction between differentially high unemployment rates that represent "normal" frictional unemployment and those which are higher than the normal frictional amount. Thus his calculations lead him to the conclusion that the relatively high unemployment rates for white male teenagers are "a normal consequence of the process of looking for jobs and are not an indication of a special problem for teenagers" (*ibid.*, p. 392). The much higher rates for black teenagers of both sexes represent unnecessarily high unemployment — higher than "normal frictional" unemployment.

other industries but choose not to do so. The blacks and the unskilled laborers lack this mobility; they cannot change the color of their skin or suddenly acquire new skills. Also, the causes of high turnover rates, particularly for the blacks, are quite different from those affecting construction workers.[16] Finally, different factors are responsible for the average time spent in job search by each of the two groups.

Hence I would prefer to retain the distinction between frictional and structural unemployment, while granting that both types result from the interaction of turnover rates and search time. On an earlier occasion, I wrote that the notion of structural unemployment implied two essential conditions: (1) some degree of labor immobility along one or more dimensions of the labor force (age, sex, color, occupation, etc.); and (2) in some or all of these sectors with impaired mobility, unemployment exceeds available vacancies even when there is no deficiency of aggregate demand.[17] I should now be inclined to relax the second criterion. Structural unemployment may exist in a sector with persistently above-average unemployment, even if vacancies equal unemployment, provided that workers cannot freely move out of that sector to others with lower unemployment rates when and if they wish to do so. The above-average unemployment in this sector of the labor market may be due to above-average quit rates (because of low wages or unsatisfactory working conditions broadly defined) or longer-than-average search time between jobs. The important fact is that the worker has little or no opportunity to move out of that particular labor market. Sex and color place absolute barriers on mobility if the labor market is classified by these characteristics. Age changes only with the passage of time. Mobility is possible among occupations, though more so among some than among others. It is possible to move among industries. Geographical mobility is characteristic of the United States, although we are all familiar with the problem of depressed areas and with less extreme examples of significant geographical differentials in unemployment rates.

In short, immobility is the essential feature of a segmented labor market characterized by a significant dispersion of unemployment rates among sub-

[16]Doeringer, Piore, and other young economists have developed the "dual labor market" hypothesis to explain the relatively high unemployment and low wages of nonwhites and other underprivileged groups. See, for example, Peter Doeringer and Michael Piore, *Internal Labor Markets and Manpower Analysis* (Indianapolis: D. C. Heath, 1971), chap. 8; the papers by Michael Piore, Harold M. Baron and Bennett Hymer, and Barry Bluestone in *Problems in Political Economy: An Urban Perspective*, ed. David M. Gordon (Indianapolis: D. C. Heath, 1971), pp. 90–107; and Department of Labor, *Manpower Report of the President*, April 1971, pp. 96–98. These sources contain additional references to the relevant literature.

[17]Gordon, *The Goal of Full Employment*, p. 57.

markets.[18] Some part of this dispersion may be due to relatively high rates of job turnover associated with the production processes involved — i.e., contract construction or agriculture's need for harvest labor. Some unemployment rates may be above the national average because of longer-than-average search periods caused by particularly poor information that impedes the prompt matching of job leavers or new entrants with available vacancies. If the relatively high unemployment rates resulting from such above-average job turnover or time spent in search are offset by relatively high wages or other attractions so that workers do not move to other labor submarkets, even though they are free to do so, then I should say that these high rates are due to differentially high frictional unemployment. If the relatively high rate of job turnover and length of search are not sufficienctly offset by other advantages, including higher wages, so that workers want to move to other sectors of the labor market but cannot, then I should classify the excess of unemployment over some "normal" frictional amount as "structural unemployment" — even though vacancies might equal unemployment in that particular sector of the labor market.

Following up on this line of reasoning, we may say that the position of the Phillips curve depends on (1) "normal" frictional unemployment, however defined; (2) differentially high frictional unemployment in some markets which is offset by relatively high wages or other attractions of the job, but with workers choosing not to move to other submarkets, although they are able to do so; and (3) two types of "structural" unemployment — (a) differentially high frictional unemployment (with vacancies equal to, or greater than, unemployment) which is not offset by higher wages or other attractions of the job, but where workers are not able to move to other submarkets, and (b) relatively high unemployment resulting from vacancies being less than unemployment in a particular sector of the labor market even though vacancies equal or exceed unemployment in the entire economy, again with no offsetting attractions such as higher wages and with workers unable to move to sectors with lower unemployment rates.

Clearly, each of these types of unemployment calls for different remedies. The first two types encompass what is usually referred to as frictional unemployment. To reduce these two types of unemployment, it is not necessary or desirable either to expedite mobility among sectors of the labor market where this is physically possible (as among occupations or industries) or to seek to

---

[18]This is not to deny that unemployment rates in some submarkets may remain high, even with perfect mobility. This raises the question of the relation between differential unemployment rates and differences in wages. For brief consideration of this question with respect to geographical differentials, see Hall, "Why Is the Unemployment Rate So High at Full Employment?"

eliminate the basis of market segmentation (as by sex or color). What is needed is a reduction of job turnover and of search time — in all sectors and particularly in those in which turnover and search time are above the national average. This might even be accompanied by a deceleration in the rate of wage increases in these sectors during the period in which such frictional unemployment was being reduced. Reducing the two types of structural unemployment under my third heading, on the other hand, calls for improving mobility among the different sectors of the labor market where this is physically possible, or for reducing or abolishing the basis of market segmentation (as by sex, color, or age), and thus for consolidating particular submarkets into larger sectors.

Manpower policy can probably make its greatest contribution to shifting the Phillips curve by seeking to reduce the two types of structural unemployment that I have described. But it can also help to reduce the two types of frictional unemployment by bringing about a decline in turnover rates and search time in particular sectors, without increasing mobility among sectors or trying to eliminate the boundaries that divide the different sectors of the labor market.

Thus far, my emphasis has been on reducing unemployment in particular sectors of the labor market in which it is particularly high. This tends to be the approach in discussions of how manpower policy may help to shift the Phillips curve to the left. It is increasingly coming to be realized, however, that the curve can also be shifted by concentrating on the sectors in which unemployment is particurlarly low. In sectors characterized by labor shortages — where vacancies exceed unemployment — wages are likely to rise particularly rapidly, and such wage increases and attendant price increases tend to spill over into other sectors, even those in which unemployment exceeds vacancies. This spillover effect has received considerable attention in the last few years, although the phenomenon had been recognized earlier.[19]

This suggests that manpower programs need to pay more attention than they now do to upgrading the skills of those who can most readily move into the areas of skill shortages. This includes upgrading the *employed* as well as the unemployed. Unfortunately, the most disadvantaged workers, on whom present manpower programs concentrate, are not necessarily the best candidates for training and upgrading in order to reduce skill shortages. A corollary

[19]This effect has been emphasized by Charles Holt and his colleagues at the Urban Institute. See, for example, Holt *et al.*, *The Unemployment-Inflation Dilemma, A Manpower Solution*, their essay in the present volume, and an earlier paper of theirs, "Manpower Programs to Reduce Inflation and Unemployment: Manpower Lyrics for Macro Music," Institute Paper 350-28, The Urban Institute, November 1971. The same idea underlies the study by Otto Eckstein and Thomas Wilson, "The Determination of Money Wages in American Industry," *Quarterly Journal of Economics*, 71 (August 1962): 379–414.

of this suggestion is that manpower policy may improve the inflation-unemployment trade-off by *increasing* unemployment in some sectors (a corollary of reducing relatively high vacancy-unemployment ratios), provided that unemployment in some other sectors is correspondingly reduced.

REDUCING FRICTIONAL UNEMPLOYMENT

Reference has been made to three types of frictional unemployment: (1) some notion of "normal" frictional unemployment; (2) above-average frictional unemployment in some sectors, this differential unemployment being offset from the point of view of the worker by higher wages or other attractions of the job; and (3) above-average frictional unemployment in some sectors, involving relatively high job turnover rates and/or unusually long search time, where offsetting advantages do not exist and workers are not free to move to other submarkets. I prefer to call this third type a form of structural unemployment.

Reducing frictional unemployment, whether normal or above normal, involves reducing job turnover and search time.[20] Let us first consider frictional unemployment caused by other than seasonal factors. Most suggestions have to do with reducing search time, and in this country substantial efforts have already been made to improve the quality, and to extend the services, of the federal-state employment service. Much more still needs to be done. Specific manpower programs concerned with counseling, training, and remedial education also serve to reduce search time and the quit rate, and here again there is much room for further progress.

With respect to teenagers and young adults, the problem is much more the frequency of job changes than the length of time spent between jobs. Turnover rates are high for this group, particularly for the teenagers. The public schools, and especially the high schools, have so far failed to do what needs to be done to reduce future turnover rates (and search time) for both graduates and dropouts — better counseling and closer contacts with the local employment service and local employers; more relevant vocational training; providing stronger stimuli to students to absorb general education; etc. This is a familiar story.[21]

[20]To be accurate, I should point out that not only job leavers but also new entrants into the labor force add to the gross flow into unemployment. In the United States, the number of persons experiencing some unemployment in a given year tends to run 10 or more times higher than the average number unemployed during the year. In a prosperous year, the average spell of unemployment is about five weeks. See Hyman B. Kaitz, "Analyzing the Length of Spells of Unemployment," *Monthly Labor Review*, November 1970, pp. 11–20.

[21]Some recent encouraging developments in the field of vocational education are reported in *Business Week*, July 31, 1971.

The contribution to total unemployment resulting from frequent job shifting by younger members of the labor force should not, however, be exaggerated. While job leavers contributed 1.5 percentage points to the teenage unemployment rate of 12.7 percent in 1968, in contrast to only 0.5 percentage point for all unemployed, they accounted for only 11.6 percent of total teenage unemployment, a smaller percentage than that for all unemployed workers. The great bulk of teenage unemployment (about 73 percent in 1968) consists of new entrants and re-entrants into the labor force. More than half of these in 1968 wanted only temporary work.[22]

The position of adult women is, as might be expected, intermediate between that of adult males and that of teenagers. Nearly half of adult female unemployment in 1968 consisted of new workers and re-entrants, with slightly more than half being job losers or job leavers.[23]

All told, in the prosperous year 1968, nearly half the unemployed apparently consisted of entrants into the labor force — and were overwhelmingly women and teenagers. Reducing this component of frictional unemployment involves a reduction in search time — or, alternatively, methods of discouraging the large flow into the labor force of temporary and part-time workers. The latter is hardly an acceptable alternative. But, in the absence of a significant shortening of the average search period, this large flow means that we must accept a significant amount of frictional unemployment over and above that resulting from job turnover among permanent members of the labor force.

In 1968, a bit more than half of the unemployed consisted of job losers (38 percent) and job leavers (about 15 percent). For unemployed males aged twenty and over, 60 percent were job losers and another 17 percent had voluntarily left their last job.[24] Some fraction of the job losses resulted from inadequate qualifications and from a mismatching of workers and jobs. These figures suggest that manpower policy can contribute something to reducing the job turnover rate. The opportunities here are heavily concentrated among youth and underprivileged minority groups, among whom dissatisfaction with present jobs may be quite prevalent. And, of course, for any given rate of job turnover, frictional unemployment can be further reduced by a better flow of information that reduces the average time spent in job search.

It should be added that improved labor market information may serve to *increase* the turnover rate among some groups of workers, while reducing it among others. To the extent that a better matching of workers and jobs is achieved, the number of early quits and the turnover rate are reduced. But

[22]Kathryn D. Hoyle, "Job Losers, Leavers, and Entrants: A Report on the Unemployed," *Monthly Labor Review*, April 1969, pp. 25, 27.

[23]*Ibid.*, p. 25.

[24]*Ibid.*

better information about available vacancies, under conditions of high employment, is likely to increase the number of voluntary quits among better-qualified and otherwise mobile workers.[25]

One may merely note in passing that anything that can be done to regularize casual work — as among longshoremen — will reduce turnover and frictional unemployment. Some progress has been made in this direction in the United States and in other countries.[26]

Let us turn now to seasonal unemployment, about which much too little has been done in the United States, in contrast to some other countries.[27] Using a method previously developed by the Bureau of Labor Statistics, I have made a rough estimate of the amount of seasonal unemployment in the United States in 1969.[28] The calculation suggests that seasonal unemployment accounted for about one-fifth of total unemployment in 1969, or about 0.7 of the total unemployment rate of 3.5 percent.[29] Insofar as it is safe to make comparisons with an earlier year like 1960, in view of changes that have occurred in the data, there was some modest reduction in the seasonal fraction of total unemployment among experienced workers in the private nonfarm sector, but a large part of this improvement was offset by the sharp increase in the proportion of total unemployment among those without previous work experience, for whom seasonal unemployment is very high.[30] The largest single contribution to seasonal unemployment in 1969 was made by those with no previous work experience — nearly a quarter of the total; the second-largest contribution was made by construction workers.

[25] An effectively functioning labor market that provides equal wages and working conditions for all workers with the same qualifications implies a high degree of labor mobility – i.e., of actual or potential turnover. But it is also essential for such a well-functioning labor market that search time be short.

[26] See Organization for Economic Cooperation and Development (OECD), *Employment Stabilization in a Growth Economy*, supplement to the final report of an international conference held October 24–27, 1967 (Paris: OECD, 1968), pp. 85ff.

[27] See, for example, Jan Wittrock, *Reducing Seasonal Unemployment in the Construction Industry* (Paris: OECD, 1967); *Employment Stabilization in a Growth Economy*, pp. 85ff.; U.S. Bureau of Labor Statistics, *Seasonality and Manpower in Construction*, BLS Bulletin no. 1642 (Washington, D.C., 1970).

[28] U.S., Congress, Joint Economic Committee, Subcommittee on Economic Statistics, *Unemployment: Terminology, Measurement, and Analysis* (Washington, D.C.: Government Printing Office, 1961). See also U.S., Bureau of Labor Statistics, *The Extent and Nature of Frictional Unemployment*, Study Paper no. 6, in U.S., Congress, Joint Economic Committee, *Study of Employment, Growth, and Price Levels* (Washington, D.C.: Government Printing Office, 1959). Seasonal indices for the 1960s were kindly supplied by the Bureau of Labor Statistics.

[29] This is essentially the same as an estimate of 20.4 percent of total unemployment for 1968 reported in Bureau of Labor Statistics, *Seasonality and Manpower in Construction*, p. 101.

[30] The Bureau of Labor Statistics estimated seasonal unemployment at a bit more than 30 percent of total unemployment for this group in 1968 (*ibid.*).

Clearly, we ought to proceed vigorously to reduce seasonal unemployment in construction. Other countries have already shown the way. Programs can also be developed with firms and trade associations to reduce costly seasonal unemployment in other industries. And what we have already suggested regarding shortening search time for teenagers and young adults would reduce seasonal unemployment for those with no previous work experience. We have seen what a large contribution this group makes to total seasonal unemployment.

If we could reduce seasonal unemployment by only a fourth, this should permit us to achieve an unemployment rate of 3.8 percent, and with presumably no more inflationary pressure than that now associated with an unemployment rate of 4 percent. There would be other substantial benefits as well.

How high is total frictional (including seasonal) unemployment in the United States today? The estimates available range from about 3 percent down to a little over 2 percent.[31] The 3 percent figure includes some unemployment that I call structural, resulting from above-average rates of turnover and/or longer-than-average search time among such groups as teenagers, young adults, blacks, and the unskilled generally. If the figure is around 3 percent, or perhaps a bit less, a persistent effort at non-prohibitive cost ought to bring unemployment down to 2.5 percent or slightly less during the 1970s. A third or more of this decline might come from a reduction in seasonal unemployment.

STRUCTURAL UNEMPLOYMENT

I have already suggested a definition of structural unemployment. Structural unemployment exists in particular sectors of the labor market having differentially high unemployment rates when these differentials are not offset by relatively high wages or other advantages and workers find it difficult or

---

[31] See, for example, Gordon, *The Goal of Full Employment*, p. 189. Arthur Ross, when commissioner of labor statistics, estimated that frictional (including seasonal) unemployment corresponded to an unemployment rate of 2-2½ percent ("Theory and Measurement of Labor Shortages," in *Critical Issues in Employment Policy* [Princeton: Princeton University, Industrial Relations Section, 1966], p. 25). Robert Hall, in "Why Is the Unemployment Rate So High at Full Employment?" suggests some figures for normal turnover rates and search time for teenagers and adults that imply a rate of frictional unemployment a bit above 3 percent. In estimating how much unemployment might be reduced by a much expanded and more effective manpower program, I arrived at a total unemployment rate of 3 percent. This, however, still contained some elements of structural unemployment as I have defined the term. (See Gordon, *The Goal of Full Employment*, pp. 168-74.) Lester Thurow has estimated that frictional unemployment in 1966 fell in the range of 2.7-3.2 percent. See his "The Role of Manpower Policy in Achieving Aggregate Goals," in *Toward a Manpower Policy*, ed. R. A. Gordon (New York: Wiley, 1967), pp. 78-81.

impossible to move to sectors with lower unemployment rates. Immobility is an essential feature of this definition.

Wide dispersion of sectoral unemployment rates suggests the existence of structural unemployment as I have defined that term. It becomes more than a suggestion if the relatively high unemployment rates are not accompanied by relatively high wages *and* if there is evidence of seriously impaired mobility out of these submarkets with relatively high unemployment. As we all know, the national labor force is segmented along a number of different dimensions — occupation, industry, geographical area, education, age, sex, color, and others. Of course, these dimensions overlap. The collection of occupations officially designated as "professional and technical" excludes the poorly educated and teenagers; white males aged twenty-five and over make up a much larger fraction of "managers, officials, and proprietors" than they do of the entire labor force; etc.

Manpower programs in the United States (and in other countries) have been chiefly concerned with reducing differentially high unemployment rates in particular labor submarkets. In the terms that I have been using, manpower policy has sought to reduce structural unemployment by: (1) improving mobility between submarkets when such mobility is possible, as from unskilled to skilled occupations or from one geographical area to another; and (2) increasing and broadening the range of employment opportunities available to particular sectors of the labor force when the distinguishing features of these sectors — such as color or sex — cannot be eliminated.

The first of these methods of reducing structural unemployment involves moving workers from sectors with relatively high unemployment rates to sectors in which unemployment rates are lower. The second method involves making vacancies available to particular categories of the unemployed who were previously not eligible — e.g., women, blacks, or those who could not pass specified tests.

While American manpower policy has not ignored job shortages in sectors with relatively high vacancy-unemployment ratios, attention has been heavily concentrated on submarkets in which unemployment has been relatively high. And in terms of my categories, manpower programs as usually defined have concentrated on accelerating mobility from high-unemployment submarkets to low-unemployment submarkets. Where mobility has not been possible — as between sectors of the labor force classified by sex and color — attention has been concentrated on increasing the number of vacancies for which members of these groups are eligible. This has been done in three ways, the most important of which is not usually thought of as a form of manpower policy — i.e., civil rights legislation and programs aimed at reducing job discrimination on the basis of color or sex. The other two types of specific manpower policies have sought (1) to reduce unemployment in particular age-sex-color groups by improving mobility along some other dimensions of the labor force, as by improving skills (including such minimal skills as steady work habits); and (2) to induce employers to alter recruiting practices and job specifications so that members of particular age-sex groups and those with a relatively low level of education and skill can qualify for jobs for which they were not formerly eligible, even without any improvement in their occupational skills.

THE DISPERSION OF UNEMPLOYMENT RATES

In studying the changing patterns of unemployment in the United States, I have made use of a measure of dispersion of unemployment rates when the labor force is classified in a particular way — e.g., by age, sex, color, or occupation. Very briefly, this measure is the ratio of a weighted average deviation of sectoral unemployment rates to the national unemployment rate. It can also be thought of as the sum of the absolute differences between each sector's share of total unemployment and its share of the labor force.[32] The larger this measure, the wider the relative dispersion of sectoral unemployment rates. It is a major objective of manpower policy to reduce such dispersion when the labor force is classified in particular ways.

Recent research suggests that the behavior of this or some similar dispersion measure — particularly when the labor force is classified by age and sex — affects the position of the Phillips curve.[33] This is to be expected. As I indicated earlier, the more the labor force is segmented and the wider the dispersion of the vacancy-unemployment ratio is among the different segments, the greater will be the rise in wages for any rate of total unemployment. The suggested dispersion measure uses the unemployment rate, rather than the unemployment-vacancy ratio, for each sector. The unemployment rate in a particular labor submarket may be relatively high either because the ratio of unemployment to vacancies is high or because the turnover rate is high or the average search period is relatively long, even though vacancies equal unemployment in that sector. In either case, relatively high unemployment which persists for particular parts of the labor force suggests structural unemployment, in the sense in which I am using the term.

---

[32] For a detailed description of this measure, see Gordon, *The Goal of Full Employment*, pp. 92–96.

[33] See George L. Perry, "Changing Labor Markets and Inflation," in *Brookings Papers on Economic Activity*, 1970, no. 3, pp. 411–41; Robert J. Gordon, "Inflation in Recession and Recovery," in *ibid.*, 1971, no. 1, pp. 105–58; G. C. Archibald, "The Phillips Curve and the Distribution of Unemployment," *American Economic Review*, 59 (May 1969): 124–34; Charles C. Holt *et al.*, "Manpower Policies to Reduce Inflation and Unemployment," pp. 51–82 of this volume; A. P. Thirlwall, "Demand Disequilibrium in

Has the dispersion of unemployment rates, when the labor force is classified in particular ways, tended to widen or narrow in the United States?

Age and Sex

I can present only an incomplete picture here, and it is a mixed one. Let us first consider my dispersion measure (which I shall refer to as *D*) along the dimensions of age and sex. Figure 1-2 tells the story. After displaying little if any trend in the fifties (merely a pronounced cyclical pattern), *D* began a dramatic rise in 1962. By 1969, it was nearly twice its 1961 value. It is true that the absolute dispersion of unemployment rates by age and sex does not fall as rapidly as the overall rate when the latter declines during cyclical expansions (note the inverse cyclical pattern in Figure 1-2), but the rise in *D* in the 1960s was far more than could be accounted for by this fact. Thus the national unemployment rate in 1965 (4.5 percent) was slightly higher than that during 1955-57 (4.1-4.4 percent), but the dispersion measure was about 50 percent greater. *D* continued to rise rapidly during 1966-69, while the unemployment rate sank slowly from 3.8 to 3.5 percent.

This widening dispersion by age and sex during the sixties resulted from (1) a significant increase in the female share of the labor force, (2) a rise in female unemployment rates compared to those of males in the same age groups, (3) a sharp increase in the number of teenagers in the labor force, and (4) a dramatic rise in the unemployment rate of teenagers relative to the national figure. It is clear that manpower policy has not been able to cope with these changes. It has not been able to prevent a relative rise in female unemployment rates. And, despite the programs aimed at teenagers, the ratio of the teenage unemployment rate to the national unemployment rate rose from 2.57 (males) and 2.43 (females) in 1961 to 3.26 and 3.80 in 1969. These ratios fell in 1970, as they typically do in a recession. If we take 1956 as a basis for comparison, teenage unemployment rates were about 2.7 times the national rate of 4.1 percent in that year, compared to the much higher ratios in 1969. The latter were still three times the national rate of 4.9 percent in 1970.

Now that the products of the postwar baby boom are becoming adults, a relative deterioration in the position of males aged twenty to twenty-four is developing. (A comparable deterioration since 1967 does not seem to have occurred among young women in the same age group, although their relative position had deteriorated during the preceding decade.) The ratio of the unemployment rate for males aged twenty to twenty-four to the national rate edged up from 1.24 in 1967 to 1.46 in 1969 and increased sharply to 1.71 in

the Labour Market and Wage Rate Inflation in the United Kingdom," *Yorkshire Bulletin of Economic and Social Research*, 21 (May 1969): 66-76.

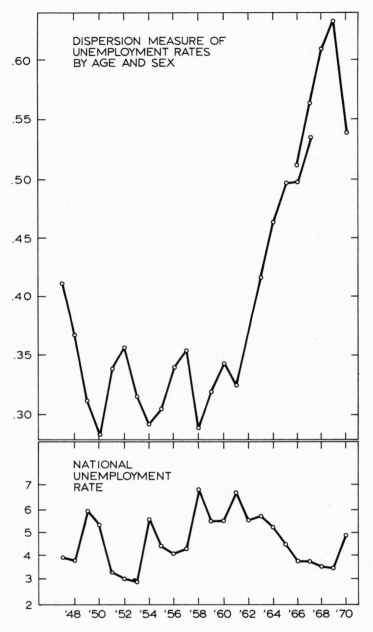

Figure 1-2. Dispersion of Unemployment Rates by Age and Sex, 1947–1970. The dispersion measure is described in the text. The original data are from appendix tables in the U.S. Department of Labor's *Manpower Report of the President.*

1970 as the national unemployment rate rose. This is higher than the ratio has been since 1958. It ranged between 1.68 and 1.81 during the boom of 1955-57.

Thus demographic factors and rising labor force participation rates for adult women have made it increasingly difficult to maintain a given unemployment rate — say, 4 percent — without generating additional inflationary pressures. A few years ago, I estimated that the change in the age-sex distribution of the labor force between 1956 and 1967 had raised the national unemployment rate by about 0.25 percent. That is, had the country's labor force had the same age-sex distribution in 1967 as existed in 1956, the age-sex specific unemployment rates which actually occurred in 1967 would have yielded a national unemployment rate about 0.25 percent lower than that which was actually experienced.[34] A similar calculation for 1970, using the 1956 age-sex distribution, puts the difference at 0.34 percent. Thus the changing age-sex distribution of the labor force has seemingly been pushing the Phillips curve to the *right*. Age-sex groups with relatively high unemployment rates have been a growing part of the labor force. Prime-age males, who in the past have had relatively low unemployment rates, have become a significantly smaller fraction of the labor force, and their unemployment rates have declined sharply relative to the national rate, aggravating labor shortages as demand expanded during the 1960s and accelerating the general rise in wages through a spillover effect.[35] It is clear that manpower policy has been able to do little to cope with these developments. The chief remedy lies in the future, as today's teenagers and young adults move into the higher age groups and increase the supply of workers in the age groups which have relatively low unemployment rates.[36]

Color

Let us turn briefly now to unemployment by race, a problem emphasized in civil rights legislation, poverty programs, and manpower policy. There has been some relative improvement in nonwhite unemployment rates in the last two or three years.[37] It will be a long, long time, however, before black

[34] R. A. Gordon, "Unemployment Patterns with 'Full Employment,'" *Industrial Relations*, 8 (October 1968): 50.

[35] In 1956, the unemployment rates for males aged twenty-five to forty-four and forty-five to sixty-four were 71 and 78 percent of the national rate, respectively. In 1969, the figures were 49 and 43 percent. In 1969, the actual unemployment rates for these two groups were much lower than they had been during the Korean war boom year, 1953, when the national unemployment rate was as low as 2.9 percent.

[36] Prospective changes in the age-sex composition of the labor force in the 1970s are discussed in a later section of this essay.

[37] The meaningfulness and permanence of this improvement are evaluated in an interesting article in the *Wall Street Journal*, January 8, 1971. See also Department of Labor, *Manpower Report of the President*, April 1971, pp. 21-22.

unemployment rates are brought down to those of whites for the same age-sex groups. Had the average rate for nonwhites in 1969 been equal to that for whites, the national unemployment rate would have been 3.1 percent instead of 3.5 percent. Clearly, it will take a massive effort and the passage of much time before this reduction can be achieved. So far as structural unemployment related to race is concerned, efforts to reduce it can pay massive dividends in other, and more important, directions, but in the next few years they are likely to have only a modest effect on the unemployment-inflation trade-off.

Let us turn now briefly to Table 1-1, which summarizes the gains that nonwhites have made in the occupations in which they have long been underrepresented. In general, the gains made since 1957 are impressive, although the nonwhite share of total employment in some occupations is still pathetically small. In all cases, improvement began considerably before the manpower and poverty programs and civil rights legislation of the 1960s. Thus in some occupations — professional-technical, managerial, and sales — gains were about as large or larger between 1957 and 1963 than between 1963 and 1969. On the other hand, the rate of improvement accelerated markedly among clerical workers, craftsmen and foremen, and semi-skilled operatives. Thus the composite of government programs aimed at improving the economic position of blacks may have added to the supply of workers in some occupations in which labor had been in particularly short supply in the middle and late 1960s.

Table 1-1. Nonwhite Workers as Percentage of Total Employment in
Selected Occupations, 1957, 1963, and 1969

Occupation	Nonwhite Workers as Percentage of Total Employment			Unemployment rate (white and nonwhite), 1969
	1957	1963	1969	
Professional and technical	3.8	5.3	6.5	1.3
Managers, officials, proprietors	2.1	2.6	3.2	0.9
Clerical	4.4	5.1	8.1	3.0
Sales	1.9	3.0	3.5	2.9
Craftsmen and Foremen	4.4	5.2	7.0	2.2
Operatives	11.3	11.8	13.9	4.4
All Occupations[a]	10.4	10.5	10.8	3.5[b]

Source: U.S. Bureau of Labor Statistics, *The Negroes in the U.S.: Their Economic and Social Situation*, BLS Bulletin no. 1511, June 1966; U.S., Department of Labor, *Manpower Report of the President*, March 1970. The data for 1969 are for workers aged sixteen and over; the earlier years shown cover those fourteen and over.

[a]Includes those not shown in table.
[b]Includes those with no previous work experience.

Occupation

For the *experienced* working force as a whole, white and nonwhite, there was a significant decline in the relative dispersion of occupational unemployment rates between 1955 and 1966, but a modest increase occurred from 1966 to 1970 (see Figure 1-3). Manpower policy can hardly be given any credit for this narrowing in the dispersion of occupational unemployment rates, most of which occurred before present manpower programs had had the time to become very effective. Most of the improvement in the 1960s reflected the fact that, with rapidly expanding demand, particularly in manufacturing, blue-collar unemployment declined more rapidly than did that of white-collar workers. Even so, my dispersion measure for experienced workers does seem to have moved to a lower level at the end of the 1960s compared to the 1950s, even at comparable overall unemployment rates.

This improvement, however, has been largely offset by the increasing proportion of the unemployed made up of those without previous work experience (who are excluded from the dispersion measure presented in Figure 1-3). The percentage of total unemployment made up of those with no prior job experience reached its postwar low in 1953; it then rose steadily to a peak in 1966; it has since declined moderately, in part because of the draft and enrollment in manpower programs for youth.[38] However, the country has also begun to experience a decline in the rate of increase in the teenage labor force that will become quite marked in the 1970s. This trend would reinforce the beneficial effect of any further decline in the relative dispersion of unemployment by occupation, should that occur in the 1970s. This projected trend, however, does not remove the need to improve and enlarge present manpower efforts directed toward youth.

LABOR FORCE PARTICIPATION

I shall not attempt to extend this survey of recent changes in the dispersion of unemployment rates to other dimensions of the labor force. Instead, let us proceed to a related topic — namely, trends in labor force participation and the extent to which conclusions based on observed patterns of unemployment rates need to be modified to allow for differential trends in participation rates.

As is well known, labor force participation rates have been declining for older men — and rising for adult women.[39] For white men aged fifty-five to sixty-four, the participation rate declined from 87.9 percent in 1959 to

[38] The effect of the Neighborhood Youth Corps and College Work Study programs on reported unemployment is discussed briefly at a later point.

[39] For age groups above thirty-five years, the rise in female labor force participation rates in the 1960s was confined to whites.

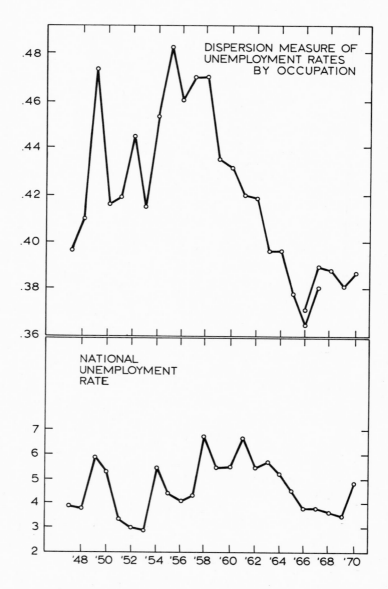

Figure 1-3. Dispersion of Unemployment Rates by Occupation, 1947–1970.
The dispersion measure is described in the text. The original data
are from appendix tables in the U.S. Department of Labor's
Manpower Report of the President.

83.9 percent in 1969. A moderate decline from 96.3 to 95.1 percent, occurred in the forty-five to fifty-four age group — and a still smaller decrease (0.6 percentage point) occurred in the thirty-five to forty-four group. Participation rates for nonwhite males between the ages of twenty-five and sixty-four have regularly been below those of whites of the same age, and they have declined considerably faster than the rates for whites during the last decade. The decline has been significant even for nonwhites in the twenty-five to forty-four age group.

Comparable differential trends in participation rates are observed if the labor force is classified by years of schooling completed. While unemployment rates for the poorly educated have not shown any significant tendency to rise relative to the national rate, participation rates have declined relative to rates for the better educated. This has been particularly true for older men. This contrast holds for whites and nonwhites taken separately.[40]

Differentially low and falling participation rates for disadvantaged sectors of the labor force led to what is generally referred to as hidden or disguised unemployment. To the extent that differentially high unemployment rates led to differentially low participation rates, "structural" unemployment is higher than the official unemployment statistics suggest, and the Phillips curve is farther to the right than it seems to be when only officially reported unemployment is recorded on the horizontal axis. Manpower and other programs, including the new program of public service employment, that succeed in significantly reducing reported unemployment among the less skilled, the poorly educated, and those suffering from various forms of job discrimination may also halt, and possibly reverse, the downward trend in participation rates for these groups. If disguised unemployment is included on the horizontal axis of the Phillips diagram, successful efforts to find jobs for those previously outside the labor force do tend to shift the curve to the left.

One of the outstanding labor market trends of the postwar period has been the rising participation rate of adult women. While relatively fewer women in the labor force complete four years of college than do men, significantly more women finish high school. The lowest unemployment rates in 1969 were in the white-collar occupations and among craftsmen and foremen. Women were particularly underrepresented among the skilled blue-collar workers, as well as among managers, officials, and proprietors. The percentage of all employed women who were in the professional-technical group was the

---

[40] See Denis F. Johnston, "Education and the Labor Force," *Monthly Labor Review*, September 1968, pp. 1–11, and Charles C. Killingsworth, "The Continuing Labor Market Twist," *ibid.*, pp. 12–17. Killingsworth has long emphasized that the pattern of the demand for labor has shifted toward the more educated and skilled workers and away from the poorly educated and the unskilled. For a more recent report, see Denis F. Johnston, "The Labor Market 'Twist,' 1964–69," *ibid.*, July 1971, pp. 26–36.

same as that for men in 1969, but the percentage had been rising more slowly for women than for men in the 1960s. The point of all this is that the opportunity exists to increase the supply of women in some of the occupations in which employment is expanding most rapidly or in which the vacancy-unemployment ratio is particularly high for other reasons. Between 1958 and 1969, more than 60 percent of the increase in female employment occurred in two, relatively low-wage occupations, the clerical group and services other than household. Physical limitations and deep-seated traditions are, of course, serious obstacles to significantly increasing the relative number of female workers in some high-wage occupations. But, to the extent that it can be done, increasing the supply of women in occupations with very low unemployment rates should make a modest contribution to reducing the upward pressure on wages in these occupations.

LABOR SHORTAGES

Manpower policy in the United States, as well as in other countries, tends to concentrate on reducing unemployment in those sectors of the labor market in which it is relatively high. Although the problem has not been neglected, less attention is paid to the need to alleviate labor shortages. Yet labor shortages — in occupations, areas, and industries in which vacancies are large relative to the number of unemployed workers available and qualified to fill these vacancies — tend to hold back the expansion of output, depress labor productivity, and exacerbate inflationary wage pressures which then spread to other sectors in which labor shortages do not exist.

This is an area in which I have no particular competence, and my comments will therefore be brief and rather general.[41] One impression that comes from a superficial review of some of the relevant literature is that more could be done in the area of manpower planning. There are several facets to the planning that is required. First, there is the need for short-term and long-term manpower projections by occupation, industry, and geographical area. This is a type of activity in which the federal government is already involved, but it is probably safe to say that such efforts could be expanded and made more effective. There is certainly room for greater involvement of employers, unions, trade associations, and state and local public agencies (including the educational system). Second, manpower policy can aim more explicitly than it does now at improving employer practices in various ways: forecasting manpower needs on an industry and company basis, planning in-house

[41]See Holt et al., The Unemployment-Inflation Dilemma, and the contribution by the same authors on pp. 51–82 of this volume; Doeringer and Piore, Internal Labor Markets and Manpower Analysis, passim, esp. chap. 9; Peter Doeringer, "Employer Adaptations to Labor Market Scarcities," in OECD, Employment Stabilization in a Growth Economy, pp. 261–77. The last item contains a number of additional references.

training programs, redesigning job specifications, making more effective use of the public employment service, and otherwise helping to improve companies' personnel and recruiting practices.[42]

Finally, and more controversially, manpower policy can seek to reduce the power of some unions to restrict entry into shortage occupations and also to curtail union rules and public restrictions of the make-work variety. Some local building trades come to mind first but are by no means the only examples. Certainly every effort should be made to secure voluntary cooperation from the unions involved. What I want to emphasize is that my conception of manpower policy is broad enough to encompass efforts along these lines to reduce artificial restrictions on the supply of labor and on its productivity.

All this suggests that, as part of a national incomes policy, manpower policy can play a not insignificant role in helping to restrain wage increases in some labor shortage areas. Obviously, programs to this end will not have the popular appeal or support that has been given to manpower programs aimed at helping the underprivileged move into jobs not protected by artificial barriers.

MANPOWER POLICY AND THE PHILLIPS CURVE THUS FAR

The last decade has brought a dramatic expansion in federal manpower programs. First-time enrollments in programs administered by the Department of Labor rose from about 34,000 in fiscal 1963 to 1,051,000 in fiscal 1970. By the latter year, federal funds obligated for these programs had risen to 1.36 billion dollars. Over these eight years, approximately 4.7 million persons had entered one or another of these programs. However, more than half of this total represented enrollments in the Neighborhood Youth Corps (NYC), and about half of these were in summer programs.[43]

New enrollments of 1.05 million in fiscal 1970 represented 1.3 percent of the average civilian labor force in 1969–70. Nearly half of these were in NYC. The cumulative total of 4.7 million who passed through these programs

---

[42] A useful study bearing on this range of problems is Doeringer and Piore, *Internal Labor Markets and Manpower Analysis.*

[43] Department of Labor, *Manpower Report of the President*, April 1971, p. 299. The programs covered by these figures include institutional and on-the-job training under the Manpower Development and Training Act (MDTA), NYC, Operation Mainstream, New Careers, Special Impact, the Concentrated Employment Program, JOBS (federally financed), and the Work Incentive Program. Of these, excluding NYC, the institutional and on-the-job training programs under MDTA have enrolled much the largest number, although the Concentrated Employment Program, JOBS, and the Work Incentive Program have become moderately important in the last few years. It should be noted that the figures cited do not include the larger part of the JOBS program, which is not government financed.

during 1963–70 constituted as much as 5.7 percent of the civilian labor force at the end of the period. This is a significant figure, although again it must be remembered that more than half represented NYC enrollees, nearly half of whom were in summer programs having limited training value.

Have these new and expanded programs had any observable effect in improving the inflation-unemployment trade-off in the United States? The answer seems to be discouragingly in the negative. In fact, the evidence continues to accumulate that during the 1960s, in spite of expanded manpower programs, the Phillips curve shifted to the *right*; the trade-off apparently worsened rather than improved. On the macroeconomic side, the best that can be said for manpower policy thus far is that it may have helped to prevent even more of a rightward shift in the Phillips curve than seems to have occurred.

The evidence regarding the unfavorable shifting of the Phillips curve during the last decade is fairly convincing.[44] In this connection, it is important to remember the distinction between the long-run and the short-run version of the Phillips curve. Virtually all recent empirical studies of the determinants of wage inflation agree that the rate of increase in the wage level in the short run depends on (1) some measure of overall ease or tightness in the labor market, as measured by, for example, either the official unemployment rate or some broader measure that reflects "disguised" as well as reported unemployment; (2) expectations as to the future behavior of prices, such expectations usually being taken to depend upon the behavior of prices in the more or less recent past; and (3) some combination of other variables, about which there is as yet no general consensus. Further, the relation tying the rate of wage change to the combination of other variables included is a *dynamic* one, with the current rate of change in wages depending on past values of one or more of the explanatory variables.

Thus, the long-run Phillips curve is defined as the partial relation between the rate of change in wages and unemployment under "steady state" conditions in which all of the explanatory variables remain unchanged for a period long enough for all lagged effects of past changes to work themselves out. A shift in the long-run Phillips curve thus reflects a more or less "permanent" change in one of the explanatory variables other than the measure of unemployment.[45] In contrast, the short-run Phillips curve may be continuously shifting, not only because of current changes in the other explanatory variables, but, even more, because of the *lagged* effects of past changes in these variables.

[44] See, for example, the papers by R. J. Gordon and George Perry in *Brookings Papers on Economic Activity*, 1970, no. 3, and 1971, no. 1; see also the paper by Holt *et al.* on pp. 51–82 of this volume.

[45] By "permanent" change I mean merely one in which the new value of the variable in question remains constant long enough for all lagged effects to work themselves out.

The apparent recent worsening of the trade-off between wage inflation and unemployment seems to reflect both an upward shift in the long-run Phillips curve, due to more or less permanent changes in one or more variables other than the unemployment rate, *and* the lagged effects of past changes in some or all of the variables that influence the rate of change in wages. Among the lagged effects that have caused the short-run Phillips curve to shift to the right, the most important has undoubtedly been the accelerating rise in prices touched off by the "demand-pull" inflation that began in 1966 with the sharp rise in federal defense expenditures.[46]

I should like to concentrate here on one factor that has apparently shifted the long-run Phillips curve in an unfavorable direction, particularly because of its relevance for manpower policy. This is the widened dispersion of unemployment rates that has occurred when the labor force is classified by age and sex, a matter to which we gave some attention in an earlier section. As we saw there, the female and teenage shares of the labor force have increased, and female and youth unemployment rates have risen relative to the national rate. Correspondingly, prime-age males have become a smaller fraction of the labor force, and during the 1960s their unemployment rate declined markedly relative to the overall rate.

As already noted, several investigators have found a significant relation between this widening dispersion in unemployment and the rate of change in wages. Because of this widened dispersion, apparently, a given overall rate of unemployment now results in a greater increase in wages than was the case in the 1950s.

Clearly manpower policy has not been able to prevent this widening dispersion of unemployment rates, although, presumably, female and particularly youth unemployment rates would have been higher than they actually were in the late sixties had there been no manpower programs. Where manpower policy seems to have failed particularly, so far as having a restraining effect on inflation is concerned, was in its inability to cope with the tightening labor markets that arose because of the decline in the relative supply of prime-age males. As we have already emphasized, if manpower

---

[46] Space does not permit a discussion here of the hypothesis that the recent worsening in the trade-off reflects not a shift in the long-run Phillips curve with a negative slope but rather the fact that the long-run Phillips curve is actually vertical, reflecting the existence of a "natural rate of unemployment," as argued by Milton Friedman, E. S. Phelps, and others. I find the theoretical arguments for such a natural rate of unemployment unconvincing, and I am not aware of any empirical demonstrations that such a natural rate in fact exists. In any event, effective manpower programs should be able to shift the Phillips curve to the left whether it is vertical or downward sloping. For a new study suggesting that the Phillips curve is vertical at an unemployment rate of about 4.5 percent, see Otto Eckstein and Roger Brinner, *The Inflation Process in the United States*, a study prepared for the Joint Economic Committee, Congress of the United States, 92nd Cong., 2nd sess., 1972 (Washington, D.C.: Government Printing Office, 1972).

policy is to play a significant anti-inflationary role, more emphasis needs to be placed on relieving labor bottlenecks. This means upgrading the employed, not merely finding low-level jobs for the disadvantaged who have been unemployed or out of the labor force.

This is not to argue that members of those groups suffering from relatively high unemployment cannot be channeled into sectors with relatively high vacancy-unemployment ratios. More effective programs, stricter implementation of antidiscrimination laws, and the redesigning of jobs by employers can help to move youth, women, and members of minority groups into occupations with relatively low unemployment rates. To a considerable extent, however, the problem of relieving job shortages will require a process of upgrading, in which the previously unemployed with limited job experience and skills move into the lower-level jobs vacated by those who are upgraded to higher-paying positions. As has been noted by others, it is essential that these opening or entry jobs not be of the "dead-end" variety. In terms of the dual labor market, a concept to which I referred earlier, significantly increasing the supply of workers available for "primary" jobs, given the demographic composition of the labor force, implies removing the barriers that now confine so many underprivileged workers to the "secondary" labor market.[47]

So far as I know, no overall study exists that would permit me to say by how much, if at all, manpower programs in the United States have reduced the overall unemployment rate below what it would have been in the absence of such programs. To reach such an estimate, I would have to know the previous and subsequent employment experience of those enrolled in, or otherwise aided by, manpower programs, what their experience would have been in the absence of these programs, and the extent to which they obtained their jobs at the expense of others seeking work.[48]

A much more limited effort has been made to estimate the direct effect of mere enrollment in manpower programs on recorded unemployment, given the manner in which enrollment in the different programs is treated in the Current Population Survey.[49] Thus Malcolm Cohen has estimated that mere enrollment in a range of manpower programs reduced the official unemploy-

---

[47]It is encouraging to find this range of problems being given new emphasis in the 1971 *Manpower Report of the President*; see chap. 3 of the *Report*.

[48]Considering the effects of manpower policy broadly, I would also need to take into account the effects of improved counseling and job placement activities, even when formal enrollment in specific programs was not involved – e.g., through the enlarged activities of the federal-state employment service.

[49]Persons in most programs – including NYC, College Work-Study, JOBS, VISTA, and New Careers – are considered to be employed. Those in institutional training are treated as unemployed. Those in the WIN program are treated as employed if they are placed in a regular job or are receiving on-the-job training; otherwise they are unemployed.

ment rate in 1967 by 0.4 percent.[50] More than half of this decline was accounted for by the Neighborhood Youth Corps, and some 80 percent of the estimated decline in unemployment was in the sixteen to twenty-one age group. I have sought to reproduce Cohen's calculations for the year 1969, using a broader range of manpower programs than he included, as well as some additional information on pre-enrollment status from the most recent *Manpower Report of the President.* These calculations suggest that the official unemployment rate in 1969 might have been 0.5 percent higher than was actually reported if all enrollees had been counted according to their pre-enrollment status. I am inclined to believe that both Cohen's and my later estimate may be somewhat on the high side. In any event, my estimate agrees with his in indicating that enrollment in manpower programs has had its chief direct effect in reducing unemployment among youth. About two-thirds of the estimated reduction in unemployment was caused by enrollment in two programs, NYC and College Work-Study, which consisted very largely of jobs that would not have existed in the absence of these programs.[51]

Let us assume that manpower policy did in fact reduce recorded unemployment by some 0.4-0.5 percentage points below what it would have been in the absence of these programs. This in itself did not reduce inflationary pressures; it actually increased them somewhat. Here I must distinguish between (a) building up enrollment in manpower programs and (b) the longer-run effect of an increased supply of workers emerging from these programs with improved skills and work habits.

The mere increase in enrollment in manpower programs such as occurred in the United States during the 1960s has on net balance had some *inflationary* effect. Recorded unemployment has been reduced, and the decline in unemployment, as implied by the negative slope of the Phillips curve, suggests some additional upward pressure on wages. (In addition, the expansion in manpower programs involves increased government expenditures, which add to aggregate demand.) The decline of 0.4-0.5 in the unemployment rate from this source does not, however, involve nearly as strong an inflationary pressure as would a comparable decline in unemployment resulting from a general increase in aggregate demand. First of all, the decline in recorded unemployment has been heavily concentrated in the sixteen to twenty-one age group, which already had very high unemployment rates; it seems reasonable to

---

[50] Malcolm S. Cohen, "The Direct Effects of Federal Manpower Programs in Reducing Unemployment," *Journal of Human Resources*, 4 (Fall 1969): 491-507.

[51] After reviewing all of the programs in which enrollees are counted as employed in the Current Population Survey, including NYC and College Work-Study, I would guess that perhaps a quarter of the persons counted as employed in these programs in 1969 were filling jobs that would have existed in the absence of these programs. Let me emphasize that this is just a guess.

assume that a given decline in overall unemployment concentrated in this sector of the labor force has less inflationary effect than a comparable decline which reduces unemployment more or less across the board, in tight as well as easy sectors of the labor market. The same can be said of the increase in manpower enrollments involving older but unskilled and underprivileged workers previously confined to the secondary labor market.

The inflationary effect of the reduction of unemployment brought about by the increased enrollment in manpower programs has also been alleviated to some slight extent by the fact that a modest fraction of the increased enrollment represents workers who are receiving on-the-job training or have been placed in jobs for which actual vacancies previously existed.[52]

The possible inflationary effects of the increase in enrollment in manpower programs has been offset to some degree by the emerging long-run effects of an *expanded* (in contrast to an *expanding*) set of programs. These longer-run effects are broadly of two sorts: (1) the beginning of an increased flow of better-qualified workers to fill jobs for which vacancies already exist and (2) some possible reduction in search time and job turnover rates as a result of training and improved counseling and placement activities.

It is impossible to quantify precisely these longer-run effects of an expanded set of programs on either the overall unemployment rate or the level and shape of the Phillips curve. My own impressions as to what has happened thus far in the United States are illustrated in Figure 1-4. WW' represents the long-run Phillips curve in this country at, say, the end of the 1950s. On this curve, an unemployment rate of OU_1 yields a rate of wage increase of $U_1 A$ $(=OW_1)$. Structural changes during the 1960s shifted the curve upward to XX', so that the same unemployment rate of OU_1 now yields a rate of wage inflation equal to $U_1 B$ $(=OW_2)$. The reduction in unemployment resulting from increased enrollment in manpower programs is measured by $U_1 U_2$. If the Phillips curve had remained unchanged, this reduction in unemployment to OU_2 would have accelerated the rate of wage increase still further to $U_2 C$ $(=OW_3)$. As I suggested previously, however, the reduction in unemployment occurred primarily among youth and the unskilled, so that the decline in unemployment had less of an effect on wages than is implied by the old Phillips curve, XX'. This is shown by the shift in the curve to YY', on which the lower unemployment rate OU_2 yields a rate of wage increase of $U_2 D$ $(=OW_4)$, lower than $U_2 C$ $(=OW_3)$.

The longer-run effects of the enlarged manpower programs, as they yield an increased flow of better-trained workers as well as reduced search time, is illustrated by the further leftward shift of the Phillips curve to ZZ', on which the lower unemployment rate of OU_2 now yields a rate of wage increase of $U_2 E$ $(=OW_5)$.

[52] See note 51.

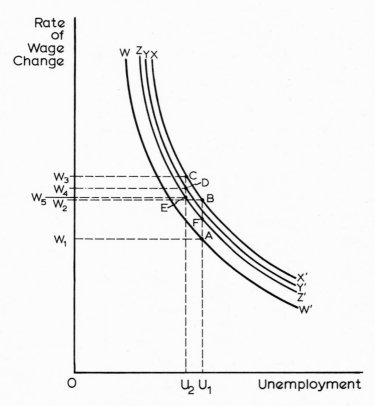

Figure 1-4. Possible Effects of Expanded Manpower Programs
on the Phillips Curve

The manner in which I have shifted the curves in Figure 1-4 is quite arbitrary. The way they have been drawn suggests that (1) structural changes did lead to a significant upward shift in the Phillips curve, (2) increased enrollment in manpower programs had an inflationary effect by reducing reported unemployment (as from OU_1 to OU_2) but also (3) led to a modest shift in the Phillips curve to the left, and (4) the Phillips curve began to shift slightly further to the left as the results of manpower programs began to make themselves felt.[53] The way I have drawn the curves suggests my very tentative conclusion (or, perhaps I should say, guess) that (1) the net macro-economic effect of manpower policy thus far has been slight (OW_5 is not much different from OW_2), and (2) we are still on a Phillips curve which is

[53]How much of a leftward shift, if any, occurred for this last reason is a matter of dispute.

significantly higher than that of a decade or more ago (compare U_1A and U_1F for the unemployment rate OU_1).

Hopefully, as an enlarged set of manpower programs stabilizes the number temporarily withdrawn from the labor supply, and as counseling and training programs, placement services, and employers' hiring practices are improved, the Phillips curve will shift further to the left without being associated at the same time with some upward movement along a given curve. This is the hoped-for, long-run, macroeconomic effect of an enlarged, effectively functioning set of manpower programs.

LOOKING AHEAD

Let us now look ahead to the year 1980. What do the prospective changes in the composition of the demand for, and the supply of, labor imply regarding the pattern of unemployment and the inflationary implications of a given unemployment rate?

Table 1-2 provides the essential data regarding the changing demographic composition of the labor force. The first three columns compare the distribution of the civilian labor force by age and sex for 1956 (the year of the lowest unemployment rate from the end of the Korean war to 1966), 1969, and as projected for 1980. The remaining two pairs of columns present for 1956 and 1969, first, actual unemployment rates for each age-sex group and, second, the ratio of each group's unemployment rate to the national rate.[54]

It is clear from Table 1-2 that some significant changes in the demographic composition of the labor force lie ahead of us. The most dramatic contrast between the 1960s and the 1970s involves the share of the labor force accounted for by males in the twenty-five to thirty-four age group. This group's share of the labor force declined by 2.5 percentage points between 1956 and 1969. It is projected to increase by about 4.0 percentage points during the 1970s. This is an increase of 30 percent and will bring the group's share of the labor force considerably above what it was in 1956. Nearly as large a relative increase will occur in the share of the labor force accounted for by women in this age group.

A significant increase also will occur in the share of the labor force accounted for by young male adults aged twenty to twenty-four. This continues a trend that has already become evident. Apparently, young women in this

---

[54]The estimates for 1980 are based on official projections presented by the U.S., Bureau of Labor Statistics in *The U.S. Economy in 1980: A Summary of B.L.S. Projections*, BLS Bulletin no. 1673 (Washington, D.C.: Government Printing Office, 1970). While the age-sex composition of the population aged sixteen and over can be predicted with considerable confidence, I am less certain about further trends in labor force participation rates, particularly for women but also for men, especially in the older age groups. This should be kept in mind in examining the estimates for 1980 in Table 1-2.

Table 1-2. Composition of the Civilian Labor Force in 1956, 1969, and
Projected to 1980, and the Actual and Relative Unemployment
Rates for 1956 and 1969, by Sex and Age

| | Percentage of Civilian Labor Force | | | Unemployment Rates | | | |
| | | | | Actual (percentage) | | Relative to National Rate | |
Sex and Age	1956	1969	1980	1956	1969	1956	1969
Male	67.75	62.21	62.17	3.8	2.8	0.93	0.80
16–19	3.66	4.79	4.66	11.1	11.4	2.71	3.26
20–24	5.24	6.54	7.53	6.9	5.1	1.68	1.46
25–34	16.06	13.55	17.60	3.3	1.9	0.80	0.54
35–44	16.02	13.08	12.02	2.6	1.5	0.63	0.43
45–54	13.53	12.81	10.23	3.0	1.5	0.73	0.43
55–64	9.35	8.74	8.00	3.5	1.8	0.85	0.51
65–	3.91	2.69	2.13	3.5	2.2	0.85	0.63
Female	32.25	37.79	37.83	4.8	4.7	1.17	1.34
16–19	2.80	3.84	3.51	11.2	13.3	2.73	3.80
20–24	3.69	5.69	6.10	6.3	6.3	1.54	1.80
25–34	6.43	6.68	8.59	4.8	4.6	1.17	1.31
35–44	7.56	7.31	6.84	3.9	3.4	0.95	0.97
45–54	6.62	7.91	6.38	3.6	2.6	0.88	0.74
55–64	3.92	5.05	5.21	3.6	2.2	0.88	0.63
65–	1.23	1.31	1.20	2.3	2.3	0.56	0.66
Total No.[a] and Average Rates	66,552	80,733	98,027	4.1	3.5	–	–

Source: Data for 1956 and 1969 were taken or computed from U.S., Department of Labor, *Manpower Report of the President*, April 1971. Data for 1980 were derived from U.S., Bureau of Labor Statistics, *The U.S. Economy in 1980: A Summary of BLS Projections*, BLS Bulletin no. 1673 (Washington, D.C.: Government Printing Office, 1970). The latter source gives an age-sex breakdown of the *total* labor force in 1980 and also a single figure for the size of the armed forces. I used the percentage distribution of the armed forces by age and sex in 1970 in order to derive an estimate of the age-sex distribution of the *civilian* labor force in 1980.

[a]In thousands.

age group will account for only a moderately larger fraction of the labor force than they did in 1969; their share will increase much less rapidly than it did during 1956–69. I might note also that the teenage fraction of the labor force has stopped increasing and will decline modestly in the 1970s — hopefully with some beneficial effect on the very high unemployment rates for this group.

It is time now to look at the continued attrition in the share of the labor force composed of workers thirty-five years of age and older. Men aged thirty-five to sixty-four comprised 38.9 percent of the labor force in 1956. This figure had fallen to 34.6 by 1969; it will be down to about 30 percent by 1980. The greatest relative decline will occur in the forty-five to fifty-four age group, just as the sharpest decline was in the thirty-five to forty-four age group in the preceding decade. The share of mature women in the labor force also will decline. Those between the ages of thirty-five and fifty-five will constitute only 13.2 percent of the labor force in 1980, a decline of 2 percentage points from 1969. The share of women aged fifty-five to sixty-four will apparently continue to increase, but much more slowly than it did during the preceding ten to fifteen years.

The declining share of the labor force composed of males aged thirty-five to sixty-four during 1956–69 was accompanied by a sharp fall in unemployment rates for this group relative to the overall unemployment rate. (See the last two columns of Table 1-2.) In 1969, when the national rate was 3.5 percent, the unemployment rate for men in each of the ten-year age groups from twenty-five to sixty-four was significantly less than it was even in 1953, when the national unemployment rate was as low as 2.9 percent. Even in 1970, with the overall rate up to 4.9 percent, unemployment rates for males aged thirty-five to sixty-four were *lower* than they were in the "full-employment" year 1956.

Assuming that the overall unemployment rate in the late 1970s is in the neighborhood of 4 percent, how much further can we expect unemployment rates to decline for men aged thirty-five and over as their share of the labor force continues to decline? For men thirty-five to fifty-four, unemployment was already as low as 1.5 percent in 1969 – 1.4 percent if only whites are considered. A good deal has been heard in the last few years about the "spillover" effects of large wage increases in sectors characterized by relative labor shortages. Apart from other changes that will be occurring, will the growing scarcity of mature workers increase the inflationary pressures associated with a given national unemployment rate?

Clearly the demand for labor in the 1970s will have to shift in the direction of younger adult workers; and the more readily it does so, the less will be the inflationary implications of maintained full employment. This calls for flexibility in recruiting, promotion, and personnel practices generally. A significantly younger labor force may also imply more labor turnover, and consequently somewhat higher frictional unemployment, and perhaps greater intransigence in collective bargaining on the labor side. Clearly manpower policy has a major task to perform in expediting this increased flow of young workers into steady jobs and in expediting their transfer and promotion into high-vacancy jobs typically manned by older workers. It is not obvious that public manpower programs and employer personnel practices are prepared for the change in the age structure of the labor force that lies ahead.

It is impossible to predict what precise pattern of unemployment rates by age and sex will emerge from these demographic changes as they interact with other forces operating on the national labor market. I shall merely add that the actual pattern of unemployment rates in 1969 applied to the projected age-sex composition of the labor force in 1980 gives a value for our dispersion measure which about equals that for 1968 — close to the highest value reached in 1969 and far above the figure for any year in the 1950s (see Figure 1-2). Unless the spread of unemployment rates does narrow significantly, the dispersion in these rates will continue to cause a given overall unemployment rate to have somewhat greater inflationary implications than was the case in the 1950s.[55]

The share of nonwhites in the labor force will expand in the 1970s, from about 11.1 to 12.0 percent.[56] In contrast to whites, the black teenage share of the labor force will increase. But, as in the case of whites, it is in the twenty-five to thirty-four age group that the supply of nonwhite workers will expand most rapidly. This is particularly so for men; according to the official projections, the supply of nonwhite female workers in this age group will grow less rapidly than their white counterparts. We have already noted the marked decline that will occur in the share of the labor force composed of workers aged thirty-five and over. This holds for nonwhites also, although the decline will be more marked among white males.

These prospective changes do not suggest any narrowing in the dispersion of unemployment rates by age, sex, and color; rather, the opposite is to be expected. And, to that extent, the changes will increase the effort required of manpower policy and civil rights programs to shift the Phillips curve to the left, not to mention the more important issue of achieving a more equitable distribution of economic opportunity.

These prospective demographic changes may be offset to some extent by continued improvement in the level and distribution of education. The fraction of the labor force with at least a high-school education will increase significantly in the 1970s, and the improvement will be more marked for blacks than for whites. The proportion of the labor force with some college education also will continue to grow, and again more rapidly among blacks than among whites.[57]

It is, of course, the younger age groups in the labor force which reflect most of the recent improvements in the quantity and quality of education. As

[55] Actually, if relative unemployment rates for the different age-sex groups react in the expected manner to changes in labor force shares, the weighted dispersion of unemployment rates by age and sex will widen further.

[56] The figures in this paragraph, as in the case of the projections for 1980 cited earlier, were taken from *The U.S. Economy in 1980*; see p. 41 of this publication.

[57] *Ibid.*, p. 42.

already noted, the largest increases in labor supply in the 1970s will occur in the age groups twenty to twenty-four and, particularly, twenty-five to thirty-four. Their higher level of education should make easier the adaptation of the labor force to the continuing shift from blue-collar to white-collar jobs and retard the rise in their unemployment rates relative to that of the older age groups.[58] On net balance, then, a higher level of education should help to offset, at least in part, the effect of demographic trends in widening the dispersion of unemployment rates by age, sex, and color.

Prospective changes in the composition of the demand for labor, by occupation and industry, have already received considerable attention in the literature. In brief, there will continue to be a significant shifting in the pattern of employment toward white-collar occupations and service-producing industries.[59] In the past, the labor force has been able to adjust to these changes. My measure of unemployment dispersion by occupation, for example, remained substantially unchanged in the latter half of the sixties; if anything, there was a slight narrowing in the dispersion of unemployment rates by industry. As I have noted elsewhere, the most serious problems of structural unemployment (as defined earlier in this essay) since the mid-fifties have arisen from changes on the supply side of the labor market rather than on the demand side.[60] These involved primarily the altered age-sex composition of the labor force and the influx of unskilled and underprivileged workers into the central cities of the North and West. The latter development helped to convert underemployment in rural areas into open unemployment and to some extent withdrawal from the labor force in the urban ghettos.

Mention of ghetto unemployment suggests one respect in which there has been a significant change in the composition of demand to which an important segment of the labor supply has found it difficult to adjust. This involves the movement of industry to the suburbs, while a significant part of the urban labor supply, particularly blacks, remains concentrated in the central cities.[61] This is a problem that has been exacerbated by growing deficiencies in urban transportation and *de facto* discrimination in housing. This, of

[58] At the same time, it may further exacerbate the employment problems of the declining number of older workers with relatively little education. This is a group which has suffered from what Charles Killingsworth has called "operation twist" – i.e., a lack of qualification for the new jobs created by technology and the changing pattern of demand. The employment problems of this group have been reflected more in declining labor force participation than in rising relative unemployment rates. For recent evidence that this "twist" was halted during the boom in the latter half of the 1960s, see Johnston, "The Labor Market 'Twist', 1964–69," pp. 26–36.

[59] See Bureau of Labor Statistics, *The U.S. Economy in 1980*, p. 42.

[60] Gordon, "Unemployment Patterns with 'Full Employment,' " p. 46.

[61] This problem received considerable attention in the 1971 *Manpower Report of the President*; see chap. 3.

course, is a familiar story – but no less serious for being familiar. Unfortunately it represents a type of problem which conventional manpower policy is not equipped to handle. And, it seems safe to predict, the problem will still be a serious one at the end of the 1970s.

CONCLUSION

The analysis in this essay and a considerable body of supporting literature suggest that a large-scale and effective set of manpower programs *can* make some hopefully significant contribution to improving the trade-off between unemployment and inflation. But that is as far as the results of this study permit us to go. In fact, because of structural changes, the trade-off actually worsened during the last decade or more, and manpower policy during the sixties was on too small and experimental a scale – and not sufficiently directed toward the problem of wage inflation – to have much offsetting effect.

Foreseeable structural changes in the labor market of the 1970s are not by themselves likely to bring about any leftward shift in the long-run Phillips curve. If anything, on net balance, the trend is likely to be the other way, in the absence of a much expanded and more effective set of manpower programs. It is encouraging that Congress and the administration, although they differ on details, are apparently inclined to move in the direction of such expansion and improvement. While the emphasis will and should continue to be on providing greater equality of economic opportunity to the less privileged segments of the population, it is to be hoped that more attention will be paid to the ways in which an expanded manpower effort can contribute to reducing the inflationary pressures associated with a low overall level of unemployment. This calls for a stronger effort to reduce particular labor scarcities, to stimulate increases in labor productivity and reduce restrictive labor practices, to stimulate more effective manpower planning by employers, to extend and improve the placement activities of the Employment Service, etc.[62]

This is not to suggest that manpower programs alone, on whatever scale, are a sufficient supplement to monetary and fiscal policy to bring about a combination of unemployment and inflation that most Americans will find acceptable. The Nixon administration reluctantly came to the same con-

[62] These rather general suggestions point up the importance of a comment by a Swedish expert in the manpower field: "One of the main tasks of research can be expressed as finding out which combination of selective measures [of manpower policy broadly defined] will have the best effects for lowering the Phillips curve, i.e., to make a high level of employment compatible with reasonable price stability." Rudolf Meidner, "Active Manpower Policy and the Inflation-Unemployment Dilemma," *Swedish Journal of Economics*, 71 (September 1969): 183.

clusion in 1971, and the country is now embarked on a program of much more government intervention in commodity and labor markets than it has been accustomed to in peacetime. But that is another story.[63]

<hr>

[63] These final comments were written before budgetary developments made it seem likely that manpower programs might be cut back rather than expanded. Also, in the light of recent experience, I should today put more emphasis than I have on the desirability of a large-scale public service employment program, with which I have not dealt in this paper.

CHAPTER TWO

MANPOWER POLICIES TO REDUCE INFLATION AND UNEMPLOYMENT

Charles C. Holt, C. Duncan MacRae, Stuart O. Schweitzer, and Ralph E. Smith[*]

INFLATION, UNEMPLOYMENT, AND LABOR MARKET FRICTIONS

Analysis of the postwar relationship between inflation and unemployment indicates the existence of an unacceptable trade-off between the achievement of price stability and full employment. To achieve a 4 percent unemployment rate, for instance, requires a rate of price inflation in excess of 4 percent per year.[1] Efforts to bring unemployment down to the 3 percent range touch off inflation rates on the order of 7 percent, and efforts to hold inflation down to around 3 percent annually generate unemployment in the neighborhood of 5 percent. Since the underlying long-run relationship tends to be concealed by disturbances and short-run dynamic responses, we do not want here to stress an estimate of the precise relation. We do want to point up the character of the problem.

[*]The preparation of this report was supported by the National Science Foundation, the Manpower Administration of the U.S. Department of Labor (contract No. 82-09-68-44), and the Ford Foundation. The opinions expressed are those of the authors and do not necessarily represent those of The Urban Institute or its sponsors. Moreover, the researchers are solely responsible for the factual accuracy of all material developed in this paper.

[1]C. C. Holt, C. D. MacRae, S. O. Schweitzer, and R. E. Smith, *The Unemployment-Inflation Dilemma: A Manpower Solution* (Washington, D.C.: The Urban Institute, 1971).

This type of relationship, found by A. W. Phillips in almost a century of British data, poses a cruel choice between price stability and full employment. We trace this unemployment-inflation relation, or Phillips curve, to various dynamic aspects of the labor market. These aspects include: (1) the continual turnover of labor flowing through the market, (2) the search required to match workers and job vacancies, and (3) the wage-price response relationship.

The problems of inflation and unemployment have been attributed to excesses or deficiencies of aggregate demand, and the policy response has been to use fiscal and monetary measures for manipulating demand. However, because this approach is inadequate, we try to identify the structural changes in the economy which should be sought, and propose programs for achieving them.

Our research indicates that the crux of the inflation-unemployment problem is that, when we attempt to increase production and attain full employment by expanding aggregate demand, frictions in the labor market progressively deflect the extra demand into upward pressure on wages and prices rather than into real output. The result is that excessive inflation occurs when we attain full employment. Our analysis of the labor market structure, however, indicates that this deflection could be significantly averted with the use of broadened and redirected manpower programs. This strategy holds promise for reducing inflation and unemployment at the same time, provided that the programs are implemented effectively and on a sufficient scale. To design effective programs, we must first identify those aspects of the economy which need to be changed.

What Needs to be Done

Job search and labor turnover are key elements that determine the levels of employment, unemployment, and vacancies. Vacancy and unemployment rates depend on the speed of placement and the labor turnover rates — more specifically, on quit and layoff rates.

Segmentation of the labor market is another key element because barriers between occupations decrease the speed of placement. Anything that restricts the range of worker and employer choice also lowers placement quality, as indicated by higher turnover rates.

This points toward the desirability of making certain changes in the operation of the labor market. To reduce the quit rate, jobs need to be more satisfying for workers, and labor market information needs to be more complete. To reduce layoff rates, work needs to be organized so that jobs last longer, and worker productivity relative to wages needs to be increased. To speed placements, search and information processes need to be more efficient. To broaden the range of market opportunities for worker and employer, barriers that unnecessarily segment the labor market need to be reduced.

In the following section, the job-search turnover analysis of the labor market is used to develop a theory of inflation which, on the one hand, explains the simultaneous existence of inflation and unemployment and, on the other hand, indicates avenues of fruitful policy orientation which will improve the Phillips relation. This section contains, as well, schematic and empirical extensions of the analysis. Next, the policy implications are presented and discussed. Finally, some specific programmatic recommendations are introduced to illustrate the measures which would be required if we were to implement a manpower strategy to improve the inflation-unemployment trade-off.

A manpower strategy to improve the inflation-unemployment trade-off appears likely to generate desired changes of these kinds. This does not mean that the proposals would be easy to carry out. Nor do we imply that other approaches are not needed. Some argue that monopoly power in the hands of employers and unions has serious inflationary effects, particularly in tight labor markets. Our reading of the evidence is that frictions in the labor market make a greater contribution to the inflation-unemployment dilemma, and we have concentrated our effort on them.

SUMMARY OF THE ANALYSIS

In this section a summary of the statistical and theoretical analyses of the model is presented. Much of the work, of course, builds upon previous studies.[2]

There is abundant evidence that the abilities and tastes of workers are complex and varied, and that the requirements and inducements of jobs are similarly complex and differentiated. Consequently a time-consuming search process for both worker and employer is required to attain employment matches that will be both satisfying and productive. Unfortunately this process often is impeded by barriers such as those based on prejudice, union membership, and hiring policies not geared to productivity. Geographic distance further segments the labor market. Once employment relationships are established, they are often soon ended by quits or layoffs, so that employers and workers must resume searching the labor markets.

In the American economy roughly one man in twenty is searching for a job which will last on the average only two years. Between three and five million workers and a corresponding number of vacancies are continually involved in this search process, and the *annual* flow through the labor market

[2] See *ibid.*, for an extensive bibliography.

is roughly half the size of the labor force. Unemployment is a costly and wearing experience that typically lasts weeks or months, and for many workers it is suffered recurrently.

In general, high turnover rates and long search times account for high base levels of both unemployment and vacancies. Some particular groups of workers have relatively high turnover rates and take longer to find jobs. This results in longer and more frequent bouts of unemployment and hence in higher unemployment rates for these groups. Since job tenure is short, these vacancies must be filled often. As a result the vacancy rates for these jobs also are relatively high.

Money wages tend to change when the number of vacancies gets out of balance with the number of eligible unemployed workers. When the ratio of vacancies to unemployment is "high," wage increases are granted to workers changing jobs; in addition, employers raise the wages of their present employees more quickly in order to hold their work forces. However, wages can be stable with either high unemployment *and* high vacancy rates, or low unemployment rates *and* low vacancy rates. Hence high unemployment rates in themselves do not indicate deflationary pressures on wages.

Increases in aggregate demand lead employers to increase the number of vacancies as they seek to increase employment and production. With more vacancies to choose from the unemployed find jobs more quickly and unemployment rates decline. There is a strong tendency, resulting from the interrelatedness of labor markets, for all types of vacancies to increase or decrease in roughly the same proportion when aggregate demand changes, and similarly for the unemployment of all types of workers to change in the opposite direction by the same proportion. Thus, fairly stable and persistent equilibrium patterns tend to occur which relate the different unemployment and vacancy rates of various groups, cities, occupations, etc.

As a result of these relationships, changes in aggregate demand tend to make the ratios of vacancies to unemployment move together in all labor markets, and this tends to put a uniform inflationary pressure on all markets so that the money wages in all sectors tend to rise together. This uniformity of wage movement is consistent with quite different unemployment rates in various market sectors.

But, when aggregate demand changes, its regional and industrial composition usually does as well, so that the equilibria just discussed are constantly being disturbed and the various sectors of the labor market must absorb temporary and permanent changes in the pattern of demand. Decisions to locate new plants and spontaneous shifts of population also introduce disturbances.

Hence superimposed on the equilibrium relationships among unemployment, vacancies, and wage change that we have just described are imbalances in the demand and supply of labor which occur in various segments of the labor market so that in particular regions, industries, and occupations short-ages and gluts of labor can and do appear. These imbalances between segments on net contribute to inflation because wages are more responsive to the excess of vacancies relative to unemployment in the tight segments than they are restrained by the excess of unemployed workers relative to vacancies in the slack segments.[3] Empirical estimates of the extent of this contribution are made later in this essay.

Of course, when labor shortages drive up wages in a particular sector, new workers are drawn by the existence of vacancies at attractive wages, and after a time the inflation-producing shortage diminishes. In the meantime, how-ever, wages on net are increased.

When demand falls, employers resist laying off highly skilled workers, so that the cutback in employment falls most heavily on unskilled, low-paid workers, whose earnings are further depressed relative to those of skilled workers.

The growth of population supplies a steady inflow of young people to the labor market; hence an extra stock of vacancies and a continual growth in employment are needed. Thus the unemployment rate and the vacancy rate[4] will tend to be high when the rate of flow of new entrants into the labor market is high.

Now consider what happens as aggregate demand is increased through monetary and fiscal policy. Starting from a slack economy, the growth of vacancies increases employment opportunities, relieves any deflationary pres-sure on money wages, and attracts increased participation in the labor force. Such a stimulating policy raises output, picks up the slack in labor utilization so that labor productivity rises, stimulates investment in capital and in train-ing, speeds the introduction of capital and labor-saving technology, and speeds up the process of promotion and job upgrading.

When rising aggregate demand increases the number of jobs, the stock of vacancies rises, unemployment declines, and inactive workers are drawn into active job search. The high-vacancy, low-unemployment market is an environ-ment in which training programs can be very effective. The inability of em-ployers to fill the high level of vacancies stimulates them to restructure jobs and train and reassign their work forces. Employers tend to compete for workers by increasing starting wages, but some vacancies are so difficult to fill that the employers probably cease searching. On-the-job wage increases are used by employers to try to inhibit quits.

Because of geographic, occupational, racial, and sexual segmentation of the labor market, it is quite possible for some segments of the market to remain tight while others are loose. Hence it is possible, temporarily, for some

[3] This point is illustrated graphically on p. 62.
[4] These rates are the ratios of unemployment and vacancies to labor force.

workers to experience high vacancies, upgrading opportunities, and inflationary wage increases at the same time that others are experiencing high unemployment and stagnation.

With further increases in demand, the ratios of vacancies to unemployment rise in most labor markets, and the upward pressure on wages is pervasive. However, imbalances occur between market segments, leading in some of them to shortages of skilled labor,[5] which accentuate the upward pressure on wages. The increased wages are passed on as increased prices, which in turn stimulate demands for compensating wage increases in all industries and lead to expectations of receiving these increases.[6] However, given sufficient frictions and resistances to changes in wages and prices, after a lag an equilibrium rate of wage and price change is reached. The *immediate* impact of any wage or price increase on workers, employers, and consumers is a change in real wages and prices with attendant consequences for standard of living, profit rates, etc., and hence is not viewed casually as just a nominal change in the value of money due to inflation. Hence, the pressures for wage and price changes and the resistance to them typically involve conflict and the expenditure of resources. *Very* high inflation rates could trigger institutional changes that reduce the resistance to wage and price changes, and this would increase the inflationary response.

Since the above tight labor market situation tends to be inflationary, the response is likely to be to reduce demand by monetary and fiscal policy and as a consequence to reduce the job stock. This lowers the vacancy rate, raises unemployment (particularly that of the less skilled workers), increases the number of inactive workers, lowers employment, and decreases the placement rates of training programs. Because of the abundance of unemployed workers, employers have less incentive to restructure jobs or train and reassign their work forces. The upgrading process slows, and downgrading may even occur.

The critical dilemma for economic policy in the United States arises because these inflationary pressures on money wages occur before full employment has been attained. This is to say, turnover, search time, market segmentation, and imbalances in the labor market prevent unemployment from reaching acceptable levels unless the level of vacancies is raised so high that inflation results. We are referring, here to long-run, sustainable relations, not to short-run, dynamic ones.

When we respond to the inflation problem by reducing aggregate demand and destroying job vacancies, labor participation falls, upgrading slows,

---

[5] Shortages of less skilled workers can be eliminated if more skilled workers are available.

[6] In concentrating on wage increases we are implicitly using a simple cost-markup theory of pricing. However, to explore the effects of structural changes in product markets or of income policies, a more fully developed theory of wage-price interaction and expectations would be needed.

growth declines, labor productivity falls, and low-wage-earners suffer most in wages and unemployment.

The regulation of aggregate demand cannot resolve the dilemma. It can only pursue the least-bad compromise and avoid whipsawing the economy by reacting alternately to acute inflation or to unemployment and bringing on the opposite problem.

By taking advantage of the lagged response of wages and prices, it is possible to have low unemployment and low inflation – but only *temporarily*. The opposite case, of temporarily high levels of both inflation and unemployment, also is quite possible, as recent experience amply illustrates. Structural changes are indicated. The question is how best to achieve them.

Concentration of corporate and union power certainly can affect wages, prices, and profits. Additional measures may well be needed to resolve our inflation and unemployment problem completely. However, the frictions that occur in the labor market are sufficient to account for our inflation-unemployment dilemma without reaching for additional explanations.

Graphical Analysis of the Problem

The preceding discussion of the functioning of the labor market and the need for new directions for manpower programs can be clarified somewhat by a graphical exposition. More technical analysis is given subsequently and in the literature cited below.

In our view the relationship between wage inflation and unemployment reflects the interaction of two fundamental labor market relationships, the vacancy-unemployment relation, and the wage response relation. Our ability to understand the Phillips curve, and hence our ability to improve it, hinges on our understanding these underlying relationships.

The first of these, shown in Figure 2-1, describes the inverse relationship between job vacancies and unemployment.[7] This relationship depends on the labor turnover rate and search efficiency. A rise in vacancies is associated with a decline in unemployment, and vice versa. This occurs because the flow of new-hire matches which is necessary to offset the turnover flow can be obtained either from many vacancies and few unemployed workers, or from few vacancies and many unemployed workers.

The second relation, shown in Figure 2-2, determines the response of wages to market tightness. The tighter the labor market, as evidenced by a

---

[7]The axes measure vacancies and unemployment in rate form with employment rather than labor force in the denominator.

For a discussion of the estimates and data plotted in Figures 2-1, 2-2, 2-3, and 2-5, see particularly equations (14), (20), and (23) in C. D. MacRae, S. O. Schweitzer, and C. C. Holt, "Job Search, Labor Turnover, and the Phillips Curve: An International Comparison," in *Proceedings of the Business and Economics Section of the American Statistical Association, 1970* (Washington, D.C., 1971), pp. 560–64. This paper estimated structural relations and derived the Phillips relation from them.

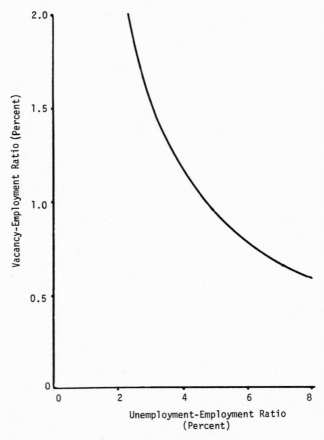

Figure 2-1. The Vacancy-Employment Relation

relatively high ratio of vacancies to unemployment, the faster wages and prices will rise. Conversely, a slack market, as evidenced by a relatively low ratio of vacancies to unemployment, will tend to be accompanied by low or negative rates of wage inflation.

Once vacancies are determined through aggregate-demand policies, the unemployment rate is determined through the *V-U* relationship, and hence the ratio of *V* to *U* is determined. And this ratio determines, through the wage response relationship, the rate of wage inflation. Thus the rate of unemployment is related to the rate of wage inflation. It is clear that a shift in the inflation-unemployment trade-off would result from shifts in either of the two underlying relationships, and this has implications for the design of a manpower policy intended to reduce inflation and unemployment.

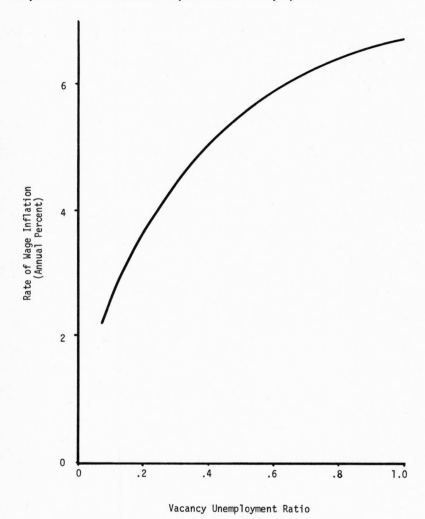

Figure 2-2. Wage Response

We now combine Figures 2-1 and 2-2 to determine the Phillips relation. We see from Figure 2-1 that when vacancies rise and unemployment falls the ratio of vacancies to unemployment rises even more sharply. This is shown on the right side of Figure 2-3. When the wage response of Figure 2-2 is plotted on the left side of Figure 2-3, we can see how unemployment relates to the inflation rate. Thus the labor market interpretation of the inflation-unemployment trade-off relation is summarized quantitatively in its simplest form in Figure 2-3. As we seek full employment by increasing aggregate demand, the reduction in unemployment requires an increasingly large rise in the vacancy-unemployment ratio, which in turn puts upward pressure on wages so that a continuing inflationary movement of wages and prices occurs.

Compartmentalization

This graphical analysis can be extended to show the implications of the curvilinear shape of the inflation-unemployment trade-off when the labor market is compartmentalized. Each of the noninteracting compartments is assumed to have its own Phillips curve. Clearly such a model is oversimplified, but the degree of interaction, or flow between market segments, may, in fact, be small enough that useful results can be obtained.

Figure 2-4 shows an inflation-unemployment trade-off. For ease of exposition, imagine the labor market to be divided into only two equal-sized compartments, A and B, each of which is subject to the inflation-unemployment trade-off shown in Figure 2-4. If the unemployment rates of the two compartments are represented by U_A and U_B, respectively, then their average (or the "national" average) will be $\bar{U}$ (midway between U_A and U_B). The respective rates of wage inflation in the compartments will be $\dot{W}_A$ and $\dot{W}_B$, which when averaged together yield $\bar{\dot{W}}$ (midway between $\dot{W}_A$ and $\dot{W}_B$). Thus the "national" Phillips curve would pass through point C, even though C lies *above* point D, which is on the curve to which each compartment individually adheres. What we see is that imbalance in unemployment rates among compartments worsens the national trade-off, for the tight area contributes to inflation more than the loose area restrains it. The strength of this effect depends on the degree of curvature of the trade-off relations. This result readily generalizes to many compartments.[8]

Thus any program which reduces the degree of dispersion of compartmental unemployment rates would tend to improve the national Phillips curve.

We have assumed the labor market to be divided into compartments — occupational, geographic, or demographic — and have analyzed the effect on aggregate wage inflation of eliminating unemployment imbalance among the compartments. This determines a maximum, potential improvement in the aggregate Phillips curve for programs operating along each of these dimensions. Whether or not this potential can be reached depends on the effectiveness of the programs in reducing unemployment dispersion.

---

[8] Where the Phillips relations of the compartments are approximated by logarithmic curves, the relevant measure of dispersion for predicting the contribution to inflation is the logarithmic average of the ratios of the national unemployment rate to the compartmental rates. A linear approximation is the weighted average of the difference between national and compartmental unemployment rates divided respectively by the compartmental rates. See pp. 68–70.

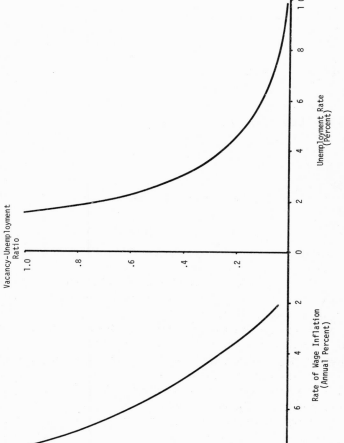

Figure 2-3. Unemployment, Vacancies, and Wage Inflation

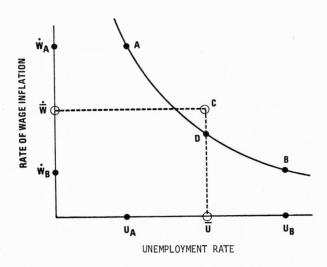

Figure 2-4. Effect of Unemployment Imbalance on Inflation
in a Compartmentalized Market

There is another way in which a reduction in dispersion can improve the aggregate trade-off. If mobility programs can improve the flow of workers from one occupational or geographic compartment to another, search efficiency and quality in matching jobs and workers will be improved. Both of these effects will lower the *V-U* curve and improve the national inflation-unemployment trade-off still further.

Finally, policies that reduce barriers between market segments will contribute to the elimination of inflationary imbalances by increasing the range of search. Thus, market segmentation influences both the vacancy-unemployment relation and the wage response relation.

The whole graphical analysis can be summarized in a figure which relates the wage inflation rate to the unemployment rate. Figure 2-5 shows that the inflation-unemployment trade-off will be improved by measures that lower both unemployment and vacancies — i.e., that shift the *U-V* relation to the left and down (to the dotted curve), and by measures that reduce the wage response for any level of unemployment (to the dotted lines).[9] With this

---

[9]The wage response relation is shown in Figure 2-5 to depend only on the V/U ratio. There may be scale effects, however, so that the wage response is influenced by the sizes of the stocks as well as by their ratio. The wage change might be more accurately predicted by a ratio with exponential weights (V^a/U^b) where a and b are constants. However, the $U-V$ curve does not shift enough for us to get a very good econometric estimate of the exact shape of the wage response function.

analysis we have tried to show the basic mechanisms by which the inflation-unemployment trade-off operates. But, more than that, we have tried to show how manpower programs can have an impact on this trade-off by altering these underlying relationships.

The Segmented Labor Market and Manpower Programs:
A Schematic Interpretation

The purpose of this section is to formulate a picture of the complex processes in the labor market which constitute the setting in which manpower programs operate.

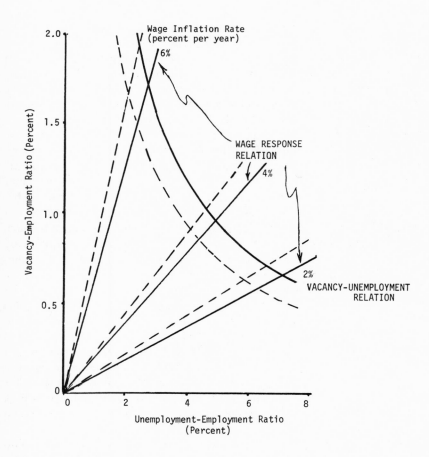

Figure 2-5. Unemployment, Vacancies, and Wage Change

External and Internal Labor Markets

In order to predict the impact of manpower programs it is essential to analyze the complex labor market and employment environment in which they operate.

Figure 2-6 sketches the major states and processes through which workers and job vacancies flow. The boxes represent stocks of workers and jobs and the processes that occur between the stocks. Most flow lines are identified by pairs of letters that indicate for each flow its source and its destination. For example the vertical line *ET* is the flow of workers from the status of employment into that of training. In order to get a feel for the relationship embodied in this diagram, we shall start by discussing the repercussions of an increase in demand which induces an increase in the number of jobs. Then we shall consider market segmentation.

The flow of new vacancies *C* enters the diagram at the lower left. (A decrease in demand, of course, would make this flow negative as the stock of job opportunities contracted.) When demand increases, the new-vacancy flow, *C*, augments the upward flow of vacancies into the vacancy stock in the external labor market, where employers search for workers. As vacancies are matched in pairs with unemployed workers by placement transactions, the new-hire flow, *H*, goes into employment.

Eventually these employment pairings terminate either by employer-initiated layoffs or by employee-initiated quits, with the result that the vacancy flow, *EV + JV*, goes back from employment to the external labor market if it is not canceled by a negative *C*, which decreases the total number of jobs in the system. A corresponding flow of workers, *EU + ET*, enters unemployment and external training. On the termination of external training, the flow into unemployment *TU*, occurs. "Training" here is interpreted broadly to include any program that "transports" the worker occupationally, geographically, or otherwise between market segments.

The stock of unemployment also is influenced by the *net* flow from inactive workers who are not searching, *UI-IU*, and by the net flow of entrants and withdrawals from the family, *FU-UF*. The stocks of inactive workers and inactive vacancies indicate that, as the result of discouragement, workers and employers have ceased to search for employment placements and are not effectively in the market. Estimates have been made of such net changes in worker "participation" in job search and hence of inclusion in the "labor force." We assume that the same phenomena occurs when employers, after a long search period, despair of finding workers to fill certain job vacancies and stop searching.

Some employed workers search for new jobs while still employed and do not quit their old jobs until they can start on new ones. This job-change flow of workers is shown as *EH*.

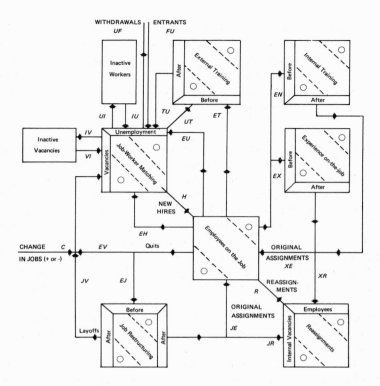

Figure 2-6. Manpower Markets and Programs

The internal labor market within the firm (on the right of the diagram) operates formal and on-the-job training. The increased capability of the worker may result in an upgraded reassignment, R, but this is not always the case. In spite of increased experience or training, some workers are left on (or returned to) their original job assignments, XE – especially when employment is not growing.

When increased experience and training do not lead to better jobs internally, workers may use their skills to gain jobs in other firms. This is one reason why employers tend to underinvest in training.

As the labor force develops through the accumulation of experience, employers may engage in job restructuring in order to keep up with their workers' increasing skills, JE, or to adapt the jobs for reassignment to other employees, JR. Also, when the structure of vacancies in the external labor market does not match well the capabilities of the unemployed workers, the employers may adapt the vacancies to the available supply by restructuring jobs JV.

The reason that the flows in the labor market are given such emphasis here is that they are surprisingly large relative to the sizes of the stocks. For example, the total annual flow of separations is almost half the size of employment. Indeed, the relationships that govern the flows, together with the externally given stocks of jobs and labor force, determine levels of employment, unemployment, and vacancies.

Market Segmentation

It is essential to recognize that workers are highly differentiated by skill, ability, experience, location, preference, race, and sex. Similarly, jobs are highly differentiated by skill requirements, inducements, location, and perhaps extraneous restrictions. As a result, it is useful to distinguish among *many* classes of workers (symbolically $m = 1, 2, \ldots, M$) and *many* classes of jobs ($n = 1, 2, \ldots, N$) in the various activities in the labor market system. The interactions in the labor market that are influenced by these factors have the effect of segmenting the market. Hiring, reassignment, employment, and separation inherently involve worker-job pairing. The behavior of a pair can be analyzed in terms of its composition — i.e., a worker of type m and a job of type n. Hence it is useful to think about these activities in terms of rectangular arrays identified by type of worker and type of job. For example, Figure 2-7 shows a segmented array of workers paired with jobs in the employment relation.

Training, experience, and restructuring involve "transformations" of workers or jobs from one type to another. That is, such activities involve transitions from one kind of worker to another, or from one kind of job to another. For example, Figure 2-8 shows the transition of workers from one category before training (row) to another category after (column), where the transition is expressed in probability terms.[10]

The stocks of inactive workers and inactive vacancies involve only the worker or the job classifications. Except for these two stocks, all of the boxes in Figure 2-6 involve row and column identifications that correspond to various worker and job types.

To illustrate the significance of segmentation we shall examine the market search and hiring process a bit more deeply. If the workers and vacancies are ordered in terms of their geographic and occupational "closeness" to each other, with "high" skill on one end, and "low" skill on the other end, of the m and n classes, we would expect to find most of the placements resulting from market search to pair workers and jobs of "similar" skill levels or locations. Although possible, it is unlikely that a worker of low skill will land

---

[10] Actually, each type of training program would have a different transition matrix of this type. Health service, rehabilitation, and other types of employment-related "transformation" programs also could be described in this way.

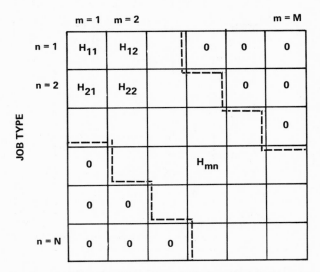

Figure 2-7. The Segmentation of Hiring. H_{mn} = the number of workers of type m hired to work on jobs of type n.

a job requiring high skill. This is indicated in the box representing the job-worker match process in Figure 2-7 by the zeros in the off-diagonal cells. It is shown more crudely in Figure 2-6 by large zeros in the off-diagonal corners.

Because of the heterogeneity and complexity of jobs and workers and the costs of obtaining and analyzing relevant information, the search and match processes involve large elements of chance; hence, relationships are likely to hold only in probability terms. The match probabilities are highest in the diagonal band, where jobs and workers are in the relevant sense "similar."

The off-diagonal zeros in Figure 2-8 reflect the fact that a *great* number of changes in occupation as the result of training are extremely unlikely, if not impossible. Patterns of zeros *within* the diagonal band, however, result from discrimination or exclusion in hiring on racial, sexual, union, or other grounds.

The productivity and satisfaction of employment matches, and hence the duration of employment relationships, depend on the interactions among the hiring, internal training, experience, job restructuring, and reassignment processes of the firm. The speed of placement depends on the interaction of search efficiency, external training, and job restructuring.

Since an analysis of the interactions among segments is not available, we shall turn to an analysis of three different kinds of dispersion in a compartmentalized labor market.

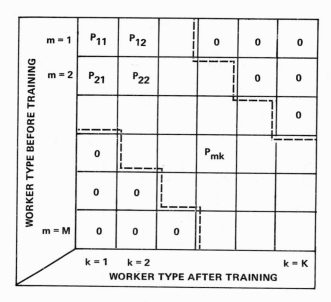

Figure 2-8. Transformation of Workers between Segments by Training.
$P_{mk} =$ the probability that a worker of type m will be
transformed to type k as a result of a particular training program.

Empirical Analysis of Labor Market Imbalance and the Phillips Curve

The manpower policy discussed in this essay is designed to reduce the dispersion of unemployment. The purpose of this section is to measure the effect of a reduction in the demographic, occupational, or geographic dispersion of unemployment on the Phillips curve.[11]

We shall begin by describing a compartmentalized model of the Phillips curve. Then we will apply the model to an analysis of wage inflation and the dispersion of unemployment.[12]

Compartmentalized Model of the Phillips Curve

Because labor mobility is high within segments of the labor market but low among segments, as a simplifying assumption we can ignore interactions among segments and postulate a compartmental Phillips relation. This relates

[11] For a discussion of previous theoretical research on the effect of the distribution of unemployment on the Phillips curve, see Holt, MacRae, Schweitzer, and Smith, *The Unemployment-Inflation Dilemma.*

[12] See C. D. MacRae and S. O. Schweitzer, "Wage Inflation and the Dispersion of Unemployment," The Urban Institute (Washington, D.C., 1972).

the compartmental inflation rate only to the corresponding compartmental unemployment rate. Compartments may be defined in demographic, geographic, industrial, or occupational terms. The national Phillips relation is then obtained by aggregating the compartmental relations.[13]

The theory of job search and labor turnover implies that a compartmental Phillips curve can be expressed in the form

$$\Delta\log(w_i) = a_i - b_i\log(u_i), \tag{1}$$

where w_i is the wage rate in the ith compartment and u_i is the corresponding unemployment rate as a proportion of employment.[14] The greater the turnover rate and the lower the efficiency of search in the ith compartment, the larger is a_i. The greater the elasticity of wage change with respect to market tightness, the larger is a_i and the smaller is b_i. For simplicity's sake we shall assume that wage elasticity is the same in all compartments, so that $b_i = b$ for all i. However, we shall not assume that turnover rates and search efficiencies are the same in all compartments, so that a_i can be different.

The national inflation rate, $\Delta\log(w)$, is a weighted average of the compartmental inflation rates, $\Delta\log(w_i)$, where the weights,[15] e_i, are the proportions of national employment in each compartment.

$$\Delta\log(w) = \Sigma\Delta\log(w_i)e_i, \tag{2}$$

and $\Sigma e_i = 1$. Substituting (1) into (2), we obtain

$$\Delta\log(w) = \bar{a} - b\log(\bar{u}), \tag{3}$$

where $\bar{a} = \Sigma a_i e_i$ and $\bar{u} = \Pi u_i^{e_i}$. $\bar{u}$ is the geometric average of the compartmental rates.

We can express the compartmentalized model in terms of the national unemployment rate as a proportion of employment, u, and the dispersion of unemployment, $Dis(u)$, by rewriting (3) as

$$\Delta\log(w) = a - b\log(u) + c\,Dis(u), \tag{4}$$

---

[13]For a theoretical development of the compartmentalized labor market, see Holt, MacRae, Schweitzer, and Smith, *The Unemployment-Inflation Dilemma*, pp. 94–101; and C. C. Holt, "How Can the Phillips Curve Be Moved to Reduce Both Inflation and Unemployment?" in *Microeconomic Foundations of Employment and Inflation Theory*, ed. E. S. Phelps *et al.* (New York: W. W. Norton, 1970), pp. 224–57.

[14]MacRae, Schweitzer, and Holt, "Job Search, Labor Turnover, and the Phillips Curve."

[15]For simplicity, employment weights are used as proxies for earnings weights in this essay.

where $Dis(u) = -\log(\tilde{u})$, $\tilde{u} = \Pi(u_i/u)^{e_i}$, and $c = b$. For given u and e_i, $\Delta\log(w)$ is minimized when $l_i = e_i$, where l_i is the proportion of labor force in the ith compartment so that $u_i = u$ for all i and $Dis(u) = 0$.

$Dis(u)$ is the sum of the relative unemployment rates in each sector, where each unemployment rate is measured as a proportion of employment weighted by the contribution of each sector to total employment. It reflects the impact of the distribution of unemployment on inflation. For in the compartmentalized model of the Phillips curve the relative unemployment rates correspond to the relative inflation rates in each sector and the contribution of each sector to total employment. Therefore $Dis(u)$ is the sum of the relative inflation rate in each sector weighted by the contribution of each sector to total inflation. If $\dfrac{U_i}{E_i} = \dfrac{U_j}{E_j}$ for all i and j, then $\dfrac{U_i}{E_i} = \dfrac{U}{E}$, so that $ln\left(\dfrac{U_i/E_i}{U/E}\right) = 0$, then $Dis(u) = 0$.[16] $Dis(u)$ will increase as the distribution of unemployment becomes more and more spread out. Note that $Dis(u)$ is not influenced by proportional movements of unemployment rates, although the variance of unemployment does change.

Wage Inflation and the Dispersion of Unemployment

Using the compartmentalized model of the Phillips curve, we can describe the relations among wage inflation and the demographic, occupational, and geographic dispersion of unemployment, as shown in Table 2-1. Wage inflation is measured in terms of average gross hourly earnings in private nonagricultural industries.[17] The measure of demographic dispersion describes only the divergence between teenage (sixteen to nineteen) and nonteenage (twenty plus) unemployment.[18] Occupational dispersion, however, is measured across the ten occupational categories within the four main occupational groups of white-collar workers, blue-collar workers, service workers, and farmers and farm laborers.[19] Geographical dispersion is measured in terms of the unemployment rates for the fifty states and the District of Columbia.[20]

[16] Capital letters refer to levels, small letters to rates.

[17] U.S. Council of Economic Advisers, *The Annual Report* (Washington, D.C.: Government Printing Office, 1970), Table C-29.

[18] U.S., Department of Labor, *Manpower Report of the President* (Washington, D.C.: Government Printing Office, 1970), Table A-3 and A-14.

[19] *Ibid.*, Table A-15.

[20] *Ibid.*, Tables D-3 and D-4. The demographic and occupational data on labor force, employment, and unemployment are derived from the *Current Population Survey* (CPS); thus, the demographic and occupational measures of dispersion are related to the national rate of unemployment derived from the CPS. The geographical data, however, are derived from estimates of Employment Security (ES) offices in each state; thus, the

Table 2-1. Wage Inflation and the Dispersion of Unemployment

Year	Inflation Rate	Unemployment Rate		Dispersion of Unemployment		
		CPS	BES	Demographic	Occupational	Geographic
1958	3.1	5.8	–	0.04	0.32	–
1959	3.5	7.3	–	0.07	0.32	–
1960	3.4	5.8	6.2	0.06	0.31	0.10
1961	2.4	7.2	7.7	0.06	0.35	0.11
1962	3.7	5.8	6.2	0.05	0.31	0.10
1963	2.7	6.0	5.9	0.10	0.33	0.09
1964	3.4	5.5	5.3	0.10	0.33	0.08
1965	3.7	4.7	4.6	0.11	0.32	0.07
1966	4.4	4.0	3.8	0.14	0.32	0.07
1967	4.6	4.0	4.0	0.12	0.31	0.07
1968	6.2	3.7	3.8	0.16	0.31	0.07
1969	6.5	3.6	3.7	0.15	0.31	0.06

Note: All rates are percentages.

There is a striking contrast in the behavior of the three measures of dispersion. Reflecting the relative increase in teenage unemployment rates, the demographic dispersion of unemployment has tripled in the past decade. Meanwhile, occupational dispersion has remained approximately constant, while geographical dispersion has declined about 40 percent.

R. A. Gordon has developed a measure of dispersion of unemployment, Du, and a measure of dispersion of employment, De.[21] Although neither measure alone reflects the impact of the distribution of unemployment on inflation, together they do, because the difference between them then is approximately equal to $Dis(u)$. To see this, note from equation (4) and its discussion that

$$Dis(u) = -\Sigma \frac{E_i}{E} \ln\left(\frac{U_i/E_i}{U/E}\right), \tag{6}$$

with all variables now measured in levels. But

$$\ln\left(\frac{U_i/E_i}{U/E}\right) \cong \frac{U_i/E_i}{U/E} - 1; \tag{7}$$

---

measure of geographic dispersion is related to a weighted average of state unemployment rates. There is a difference between the CPS and ES rates, particularly in the early 1960s. Note that all unemployment rates are expressed as a proportion of employment, not of the labor force.

[21] For an extensive discussion of changing patterns of unemployment using arithmetic measures of dispersion, see R. A. Gordon, *The Goal of Full Employment* (New York: John Wiley & Sons, 1967).

therefore,

$$Dis(u) \cong \Sigma \left(\frac{U_i}{U} - \frac{E_i}{E} \right). \tag{8}$$

Similarly,

$$Du \equiv \Sigma \left| \frac{U_i}{U} - \frac{L_i}{L} \right| \quad \text{and} \quad De \equiv \Sigma \left| \frac{E_i}{E} - \frac{L_i}{L} \right|; \tag{9}$$

therefore,

$$Du - De \cong \Sigma \left(\frac{U_i}{U} - \frac{E_i}{E} \right) \cong Dis(u). \tag{10}$$

This explains the difference in the behavior of $Dis(u)$ from that of Gordon's Du. Du by occupation fell markedly between 1958 and 1969, but this decline was accompanied by a decline in De as well, which left the difference, and hence $Dis(u)$, little affected.

By demographic characteristics, both Du and De rose, but the increase in Du was dominant. This is confirmed by the increase in $Dis(u)$.

Gordon did not consider the geographic dimension of the distribution of unemployment or employment.

Whether these trends will continue is problematic, particularly in light of the coincidence of the secular forces of growth and the cyclical forces of expansion during most of the period of our observations.[22] Nevertheless, it is possible to measure the impact of changes in the dispersion of unemployment on the Phillips curve using the compartmentalized model described above.

Estimates of the Phillips curve (3) using annual U.S. observations are shown below. Figures in parentheses are t-statistics. Significance at the 1 percent level is denoted by **. All rates are percentages.

For demographic dispersion, 1958–59,

$$\Delta \log(w) = 9.927 \qquad -3.871 \; \log(\bar{u}),$$
$$(9.684)^{**} \; (-5.912)^{**}$$

$$\bar{R}^2 = 0.755, \; S.E. = 0.622, \; D.W. = 0.914. \tag{11}$$

For occupational dispersion, 1958–69,

$$\Delta \log(w) = 9.939 \qquad -4.540 \; \log(\bar{u}),$$
$$(9.509)^{**} \; (-5.808)^{**}$$

[22] *Ibid.*

$$\bar{R}^2 = 0.748, \quad S.E. = 0.631, \quad D.W. = 0.932. \qquad (12)$$

For geographical dispersion, 1960-69,

$$\Delta\log(w) = 11.354 \qquad -4.778 \ \log(\bar{u}),$$
$$(7.557)^{**} \ (-4.892)^{**}$$

$$\bar{R}^2 = 0.718, \quad S.E. = 0.715, \quad D.W. = 0.937. \qquad (13)$$

Note that estimating a and b in (3), a compartmentalized Phillips curve, is equivalent to estimating a, b, and c in (4), an aggregate Phillips curve which includes compartmental dispersion but is subject to the theoretical constraint that $b = c$. Separate estimates of b and c in (4) were made, but b and c were not significantly different at the 5 percent level, which gives some empirical support to the model specification.

Interpreting (11)-(13) in terms of (4), we can now estimate the effect of changes in the dispersion of unemployment on the aggregate Phillips curve.

We estimate that the tripling of the demographic dispersion which occurred from 1960 to 1969 either increased the inflation rate by 0.4 percentage points for a constant unemployment rate or increased the level of unemployment by 12 percent for a constant inflation rate.[23] Moreover, a complete elimination of demographic dispersion from the 1969 level would reduce either the inflation rate by 0.6 percentage points or the level of unemployment by 14.0 percent. The latter amounts to a reduction of 0.56 percentage points from a 4.0 percent unemployment rate.

The occupational dispersion of unemployment has not changed significantly in the past ten years. However, we estimate that the elimination of occupational dispersion would either reduce the rate of wage inflation by 1.4 percentage points or reduce the level of unemployment by 25.0 percent.

Finally, the 40 percent decrease in the geographical dispersion of unemployment has reduced either the inflation rate by 0.2 percentage points or the level of unemployment by 4.0 percent. In addition, a total elimination of geographical dispersion would reduce either the inflation rate by 0.3 percentage points or the level of unemployment by 7.0 percent.

Qualifications

The compartmentalized model of the labor market is, of course, much simpler than the interacting, segmented one that we need. In spite of this simplicity, however, it appears to give interesting and relevant results.

While we have enough confidence in the compartmentalized model of the labor market to use it as a first approximation, it clearly has its limitations.

---

[23]For a similar conclusion, see G. L. Perry, "Changing Labor Markets and Inflation," *Brookings Papers on Economic Activity*, 1970, no. 3, pp. 411-41.

Two opposite and unknown biases are introduced into our estimates through the use of the theory of a compartmentalized labor market instead of a segmented one.

On one hand, the compartmentalized model does not admit the increase in vacancies and relative wages which occurs in a tight submarket to attract workers from other compartments or to induce employers to find substitutes. Omission of these important, self-correcting mechanisms will tend to exaggerate the need for skill training and mobility programs and hence will lead us to overestimate their impact. Furthermore, we have implicitly assumed that our estimates of geographic, demographic, and occupational dispersion were independent of each other.

On the other hand, in a segmented market, some institutional rigidities in the structure of wages across segments may contribute to spillover effects between segments which are absent in a completely compartmentalized market. The omission of these spillover effects would lead us to underestimate the impacts of these programs. Our judgment is that the former effect predominates, but we lack both theory and evidence on this point.

POLICY IMPLICATIONS FOR EXTENDED MANPOWER PROGRAMS

Objectives

Unemployment has long been explained in terms of deficiency in demand, friction, bottlenecks, and structural problems in the labor market. Unfortunately the latter three concepts are not well defined, nor do we have adequate tested knowledge about how manpower programs influence them or exactly what role the programs play in the inflation process. This is a great handicap in designing manpower programs to accomplish particular objectives.

To be sure, we do have enough general knowledge about these matters to implement sensible manpower programs. Indeed, some of the program recommendations that we shall make come close to programs that are currently operating. However, present programs are for the most part aimed at particular target groups that are relatively small, and at the disadvantaged in particular. The concern of this essay is with the macro objectives of inflation and unemployment, so the breadth, scale, and justification of manpower programs must be entirely different. Only now are we beginning to understand the complex, interacting system of labor markets and the inflation process well enough to specify what we want programs to accomplish and why.

Although it is far from complete, we have used the recent analytic and empirical work at The Urban Institute and elsewhere to help pinpoint areas in which programs would have maximum effect.

Without going into detail, these analyses have the following broad implications for the design of manpower programs. The level of unemployment is determined by the turnover rate, the speed of placement, growth of the labor force, and aggregate demand. Since the market is segmented by region, occupation, and demographic group, the national aggregate unemployment level is influenced by the weighted averages across segments of the turnover rates and the speeds of placement within the segments. The turnover rates of certain groups of workers are particularly high and their unemployment rates are high as well. Hence they merit special attention.

Artificial barriers increase market segmentation, which adversely affects placement speeds and qualities. The turnover rate, which determines the length of job tenure, is the sum of the quit rate and the layoff rate. These rates are influenced by, among other things, the quality of the worker-job matches.

Since the markets in which the ratios of vacancies to unemployment are especially high contribute unduly to the upward pressure on wages, inflation will be reduced by improving the balance between the regional and occupational segments of the market.

Thus, in summary, to improve the inflation-unemployment trade-off relation, we should seek extended manpower programs and policies that, on an economy-wide basis: (1) improve the speed and quality of matching workers and jobs and reduce turnover; (2) reduce the unemployment rates of groups with the highest burden now; (3) relieve labor shortages in occupational markets that are excessively tight; (4) promote geographic mobility of the labor force; and (5) reduce institutional barriers that interfere with the functioning of the labor market. Programs directed at the third target may be of two broad types: the transformation of workers through training programs to qualify for skill shortages; and the transformation of jobs through restructuring to better fit the existing labor supply in order to obtain a better balance among market segments.

Current manpower programs are oriented toward the disadvantaged, and, although we give them little attention here, we emphatically do not propose a reduction or diversion of these important efforts.

Public and Private Roles

Governmental involvement in these market processes is warranted in order to reduce detrimental spillover effects that result from privately motivated decisions. Inflation produces income redistribution, which may be inequitable. In addition, the monetary and fiscal measures that are taken to counter inflation have extensive and powerful external effects on the whole economy, by decreasing production and increasing unemployment. The individual decisionmakers who contribute to inflation are not the only ones affected by their decisions.

Such gross externalities are more than adequate justification for active governmental involvement in reducing labor market friction, structural barriers, and imbalances. Stated differently, the decisions of workers and employers motivated by individual self-interest cannot be counted on to produce the socially optimal levels of inflation or of the frictional, structural, and demand-deficiency components of unemployment. Governmental concern for demand-deficiency unemployment has been recognized since the 1930s. Now the need for the government to assume responsibility in the structural and frictional areas requires the same recognition.

Weighed against the strong and immediate private motivations that determine individual wage and price decisions, appeals for restraint in making wage and price adjustments based on the public good are likely to be undermined.

By contrast, improving the efficiency of search and manpower services finds a substantial, but of course not complete, harmony of interests between the national good and private motivations.

The present structure of the labor market implies placing serious and possibly socially disruptive burdens upon many of its participants. Even in "good" times the hardships of unemployment are greater than we generally realize. The 1971 *Report* of the Council of Economic Advisers recognized the limitations of fiscal and monetary tools in achieving full employment with price stability and thus set as its target the reduction of unemployment to about 4.5 percent of the labor force by mid-1972. The most recent month in which the rate was near 4.5 was March 1970, when it stood at 4.4 percent. Tables 2-2 and 2-3 indicate what this rate meant in terms of the incidence of unemployment among various demographic and occupation groups.

These tables illustrate the failure of some groups to find work even in periods of "full employment." For example, teenagers, whether male, female, black, or white, had an unemployment rate which, if experienced throughout the labor force, would be declared evidence of a severe recession. Unskilled laborers and factory operatives had similar, although not so severe, difficulties in finding jobs within this relatively tight labor market.

Fortunately the groups with the most severe unemployment problems are not very large — teenagers account for only 8 percent of the civilian labor force, and nonfarm laborers and operatives together account for 25 percent. Yet they are an incredibly large part of the total unemployment problem. As shown in the two tables, almost one in every four unemployed persons is between the ages of sixteen and nineteen, and one in three is a laborer or an operative. For these and some of the other groups shown in the tables, there is no such thing as a tight labor market. Lowering inflation by reducing aggregate demand incurs the heaviest costs, in terms of lost jobs, on these groups. Our recommendations are intended to promote a less costly and more equitable approach to resolving the inflation-unemployment dilemma.

Table 2-2.   Unemployment Rates among Selected Demographic Groups
at 4.4 Percent Unemployment

Demographic Group	Unemployment Rate	Ratio of Group Unemployment Rate to Unemployment Rate of Adult White Males	Unemployment Level	Percentage of Total Unemployment
White Males, 20 years and older	2.7	1.0	1,156,000	31.0
White Females, 20 years and older	4.1	1.5	1,014,000	27.2
Nonwhite Males, 20 years and older	4.6	1.7	215,000	5.8
Nonwhite Females, 20 years and older	6.6	2.4	245,000	6.6
White Males, 16–19 years	11.7	4.3	420,000	11.2
White Females, 16–19 years	13.1	4.8	384,000	10.3
Nonwhite Males, 16–19 years	19.9	7.4	97,000	2.6
Nonwhite Females, 16–19 years	30.7	11.4	105,000	2.8

Table 2-3.   Unemployment Rates among Selected Occupations
at 4.4 Percent Unemployment

Occupation Group	Unemployment Rate	Ratio of Group Unemployment Rate to Unemployment Rate of Professional and Technical Workers	Unemployment Level	Percentage of Total Unemployment
Professional and Technical Workers	2.2	1.0	206,000	5.5
Farm Workers	2.1	0.9	83,000	2.2
Craftsmen and Foremen	3.1	1.4	420,000	11.2
Sales Workers	3.4	1.5	188,000	5.0
Service Workers	4.9	2.2	500,000	13.4
Operatives	6.1	2.8	1,019,000	27.3
Nonfarm Laborers	7.5	3.4	359,000	9.6

The policy options of active control of aggregate demand or incomes policies to fight inflation have been tried before. The former, in fact, is currently being attempted — at great cost. The latter's effectiveness has been the subject of much debate because its most active period of application — and ostensible success — occurred in a period of general slack in the economy. For an incomes policy to be effective, generally, either the application must be of only a short duration, or extended use must be accompanied by appropriate product and labor market structural policies. Our knowledge concerning the role of market concentration in price decisions is probably too incomplete to warrant its advocacy as a means of shifting the Phillips curve. Our labor market–oriented analysis, on the other hand, does show a clear relationship between labor market structure and inflation and unemployment, and we therefore advocate that manpower policies be applied in this area.

Some of these policy implications will be presented briefly in the next section of this essay for illustrative purposes. None will be developed fully, however. We think it important, in view of the economic objectives, to get across the large picture of the difficult and extensive structural changes that are needed. This is in sharp contrast to earlier efforts in the manpower area, where the program targets were relatively small numbers of people. To the extent that the programs needed for reducing inflation and unemployment are similar to existing programs, we are that far ahead, but in seeing this similarity we should not miss the differences in scale and effectiveness which we must now strive for.

A SUMMARY OF PROGRAMMATIC IMPLICATIONS

The model of the inflation process contained in this paper implies a crucial role for manpower programs in any effort to improve the inflation-unemployment trade-off. A more complete description of some of the specific programs which this analysis indicates should be a part of a comprehensive labor market program, together with preliminary estimates of costs and benefits, is presented elsewhere.[24] Only a brief summary is included here.

Our programmatic recommendations are designed to accomplish the five objectives mentioned in the previous section.

Matching Workers, Jobs, and Services

The employment service plays a vital role in bringing workers and employers together and services to both. A great potential exists for improved

[24]C. C. Holt, C. D. MacRae, S. O. Schweitzer, and R. E. Smith, "Manpower Programs to Reduce Inflation and Unemployment: Manpower Lyrics for Macro Music," The Urban Institute (Washington, D.C., 1971). A condensed version of the analysis and

performance in this area. The federal-state employment service should be restructured so that in each office some staff counselors and interviewers are committed to serving the needs of workers, and some similarly committed to employers. In addition, computer matching, labor market data, and analysis would be handled as service functions of the above staffs. Although this structure would put a premium on team play by all three groups, it would help to make the organization responsive to the needs of its clients and would facilitate cooperation with private employment agencies and other groups offering placement services.

In order to help motivate and guide the employment service staff in making the matches that will contribute most to the reduction of inflation and unemployment while giving special consideration to workers and employers with placement problems, incentive formulas ought to be introduced. In particular, quality of placement measured in terms of job tenure should receive increased stress in order to reduce turnover.

Currently the private employment agencies are even more fragmented than the federal-state employment service, but they have important contributions to make to the functioning of the labor market. Fee splitting, compatible standards, etc., should be established so that public and private agencies can cooperate and compete in achieving a flexible nationwide placement system which serves the needs of all occupations.

Since some employment service functions are amenable to automation and others are not, it is urgent that we develop and install a nationwide computerized man-machine system for matching workers, jobs, and services. The computer matching system would incorporate behavioral relationships to help (when scanning the astronomical number of possible matches) predict for human follow-up the few which hold the most potential of being satisfying for the worker and productive for the employer.

If the quality and quantity of the employment service output are to be increased substantially, the staff will have to be upgraded, expanded, and trained, and salary levels will have to be raised.

The federal government should take the lead in organizing, funding, and coordinating the nationwide public-private system described above to provide for roughly triple its present capacity.

Reducing High Unemployment

Some of our recommendations focus on means of reducing the unemployment rates of groups that systematically suffer a high rate — namely, youth, blacks, and the disadvantaged. Working on the unemployment problems of

---

recommendations is presented in "Manpower Proposals for Phase III," *Brookings Papers on Economic Activity*, 1971, no. 3.

youth also contributes to solving the labor market problems of the other groups, and getting youth off to good vocational starts can yield lifetime benefits.

Currently $1.5 billion is spent annually on vocational education programs and manpower programs for the disadvantaged. These programs ought to be carefully re-evaluated and redirected toward preparing workers for employment that will be more stable, as measured by reduced turnover rates.

Our high-school programs for non-college bound students, and even our vocational schools, are weak in vocational counseling. There is, on the average, less than one counselor per school, and often the counselor lacks a suitable background for the job. Because it is important to have a closer working relationship between schools and the employment service, providing employment service experience for counselors, perhaps through a summer job rotation plan, would be useful.

To help students make the transition from school to work, work-study programs in schools ought to be started at earlier ages, and employers ought to be subsidized to offer jobs to teenagers which will give them a diversity of employment experiences.

Thus, by improving the job knowledge and employment experiences of youth, we would hope to smooth their vocational orientation and reduce the high turnover rate that causes high unemployment among them.

Reducing Critical Skill Vacancies

When the occupational composition of the work force does not match the skill requirements of jobs, the imbalance accentuates the inflation process. Hence measures are needed that will recruit labor from less tight occupations and prepare them to fill the critical skill shortages.

To do this a data and analysis effort must be implemented to anticipate or, failing that, quickly identify the occupations that will be, or already are, in short supply.

To meet these needs we recommend a major expansion of skill training that would be closely tied to anticipated skill needs and quickly responsive to those that were unanticipated. We estimate that an increase on the order of tenfold in training slots (both on-the-job and institutional) oriented toward skill shortages from the present 70,000 would cover roughly all of the occupational shortages measured in terms of long-duration vacancies.

Many skill shortages can be avoided by restructuring jobs, substituting machines, and so forth. To aid in this effort the employment service should add industrial engineers and psychologists to their current operating staff.

Many skilled women, or women who would like to work and are capable of readily learning skills, are now prevented from doing so by family responsibilities. Small children could be cared for at day care centers while their mothers work, if such centers were conveniently available. To increase the availability of this service, the government should subsidize at least the construction of day care centers for this purpose.

Reducing Geographical Imbalances

The long distances between job markets contribute to segmentation and the possibilities of imbalances between segments. The travel hurdle also contributes to the employment problems of the disadvantaged. A new mobility assistance program oriented toward regional labor shortages and the disadvantaged should be established. We recommend that the moves of about 200,000 workers and their households be aided annually, which amounts to about 10 percent of the present migration flow. Such programs have proved effective in a number of other countries.

To carry out this program, an employment service that functions nationally to facilitate the geographic moves of workers is required. Furthermore, we will need to provide suitable mobility allowances to aid moves intended to help fill shortages and advance the disadvantaged.

Reducing Institutional Barriers that Segment the Labor Market

Institutional barriers in the labor market based on licensing, union membership, discrimination, etc., inhibit the response of labor to production requirements and thereby increase unemployment and inflationary skill shortages. The tackling of this issue will require the prestige of a presidential commission to study the problem and make recommendations, the objective of which will be to formulate and implement an *active* governmental policy of dissolving such artificial barriers to employment.

Since many of these barriers were carefully constructed to protect the economic interests of various employer and worker groups, it is naïve to suppose that their dissolution will be easy. The presidential commission would need to investigate the extent to which an across-the-board manpower program aimed at a general upgrading and at increasing the investment in human capital might be an essential political and economic ingredient for supplying alternative forms of employment security and for making effective the programs oriented toward the disadvantaged.

It is unhappily true that we need much more knowledge to implement fully effective programs of the type here recommended. Hence there is an urgent need for a carefully designed, integrated, and expanded program of basic and applied research, including field experimentation and evaluation. Behavioral research for the computer matching system and the prediction of macro impacts of programs are particularly high-priority projects. However, for this work to be practically effective, increased emphasis must be given to the problems of application. For example, evaluations need to be actually used for planning, allocation, and control. This may require legislative support by Congress.

It will be essential that federal fund allocations take into account the new objective of manpower programs to combat inflation.

New Departures in the Recommendations

The changes in existing programs which we are proposing are not cosmetic; they are extensive and therefore can be expected to be expensive. Preliminary estimates suggest that expenditures on manpower activities would have to be increased by something like $14 billion if unemployment without inflation were to be reduced from the neighborhood of 4½ percent to the neighborhood of 2½ percent. It is important to remember, however, that the cost of not acting in a positive way is far higher. The cost of combatting the most recent inflation spiral, using the standard aggregate-demand techniques, has been a huge, but in many cases ignored, sum. The loss of potential Gross National Product between 1969 and 1972 was projected by the Council of Economic Advisers to exceed $90 billion.

In view of the similarity of our recommendations to some existing programs, it may be useful to note the differences.

Our evaluation of existing programs is that they have not been large enough, effective enough, or targeted on macro objectives sufficiently to have an important impact on inflation and unemployment — nor were they intended to have.

In particular, manpower programs should become much more responsive to hard-to-fill vacancies and to institutional and geographic barriers. Also, more stress should be placed on the dynamic search process in terms of both speed and quality.

The better understanding of labor market friction and structure which is now emerging indicates that the indirect impacts of manpower programs in the aggregate are very important. Admittedly the job-search labor-turnover theory that is the basis of our recommendations requires further empirical testing. But this additional work is more likely to affect the magnitude of the estimated program impacts rather than drastically to alter their proposed direction.

The costs of continuing our present approach to inflation and unemployment are considerable. If we are correct, the expansion and redirection of manpower programs should become a much more urgent item on our national agenda than it has been in the past. Until we address the frictions in the labor market, the inflation-unemployment dilemma is likely to persist.

CHAPTER THREE

REDISTRIBUTIONAL ASPECTS OF MANPOWER TRAINING PROGRAMS

Lester C. Thurow

INTRODUCTION

Manpower programs can be used to raise a country's potential rate of growth, to alter its minimum unemployment rate, to shift the Phillips curve or the natural rate of unemployment, and to change the distribution of earned income. The character of the specific manpower programs differs markedly, however, depending upon the specific goal or goals. Unfortunately, the same programs will not lead to all of these goals.

What would be the character of manpower programs designed to raise a country's potential rate of growth? Such programs would focus on those who were easiest to train. Skills and individuals would be chosen depending upon the cost-benefit ratios of programs for these skills and for these individuals. Since training costs fall as an individual's previously acquired human capital rises, training would in general be concentrated on those who are in the middle and upper ranges of the skill distribution. For those in the lower ranges of the skill distribution, efforts would focus on simplifying jobs rather than on upgrading workers.

However, current manpower training programs are not, and should not be, interested in raising the potential rate of growth. No one in the United States seems worried about the American potential growth rate, for full employment in the 1960s demonstrated that the worries of the 1950s about the Russians surpassing us were groundless. A potential growth rate of 4½ percent (the U.S. rate) seems adequate for keeping us ahead of the Russian's in the foreseeable future.

What would be the character of manpower programs designed to lower the minimum achievable unemployment rate? The history of 1960s demonstrated that the American economy can reach unemployment rates of close to 3 percent through the use of simple fiscal and monetary policies. At such unemployment rates, most unemployment is caused by the time spent looking for the "right" job rather than "a" job. In this situation, manpower programs would concentrate on mechanisms for getting new workers rapidly into the "right" job and for helping old workers switch to the "right" job. All the attention would be focused on improving the efficiency of mobility in the labor market for the areas and people with the highest benefit-cost ratios (i.e., the greatest reductions in time for a given expenditure).

However, current manpower training programs are not, and should not be, interested in lowering the minimum unemployment rate. No one is worried about voluntary unemployment at a 3 percent level of general unemployment.

What would be the character of manpower programs designed to improve the Phillips curve or the natural rate of unemployment? Training programs would play a role in such a program, for they would be used to increase the supplies of labor in sectors that reach full employment before the economy generally reaches full employment. To be successful, however, such programs would need to be embedded in a massive program for altering the institutional structure of the American economy. The current inflation indicates that monopoly and oligopoly elements are so embedded in our economy that administrative price and wage increases start long before any significant portion of the economy has reached full employment. Thus programs to alter administrative powers to set wages and prices would need to come before training programs. Training programs would have no impact on the Phillips curve or on the natural rate of unemployment unless some prior actions had been taken in *both* the labor markets and product markets. Given the heavy emphasis on training and the complete absence of programs to alter administrative pricing powers, it is very difficult to argue that present manpower programs are seriously attempting to improve the Phillips curve.

As a result there is only one rationale left for current manpower programs. They must be designed to alter the distribution of earned income. But, even within this broad goal, it is necessary to specify exactly what is to be accomplished. The aim is not one of raising the incomes of low-income workers. All of the evidence of the post–World War II period indicates that the incomes of low-income workers will grow at the same rate as average incomes, without special government programs. This is what is implied by the postwar consistency in income distribution. In addition, it is important to realize that America's poverty problem is a problem of relative incomes, not absolute incomes. U.S. poverty lines exceed average family incomes in most wealthy developed countries. For both of these reasons the aim is to alter the relative distribution of income and not simply to raise the incomes of low-income workers. As a result manpower programs work as a redistributive device only to the extent that they engender income increases that exceed those of the average worker.

The American economy faces two broad income redistribution goals. Poverty is to disappear. Race or color is to lose its importance in determining an individual's income. Viewed from the perspective of income distribution, the first goal means that the fraction of the population in the lowest income categories must be reduced to zero. The second goal means that the income distributions for different racial groups should not differ significantly. Wide individual income differences may continue to exist, but there should be no systematic differences in the proportions of each group in various income classes.

Differences in the income distributions of different racial groups provide both a static picture of what must be done to achieve economic equality and a dynamic measure of what has been happening. The dynamic measure is provided by changes in the differences: if the differences are narrowing, economic inequality is declining; if they are widening, economic inequality is increasing. The pace at which the differences are changing without specific government programs is an important factor in determining the magnitude of the programs that may be necessary to eliminate economic inequality by a specific future date. If the differences are rapidly disappearing, special programs may be unnecessary; if they are slowly disappearing, programs will be needed.

Eliminating poverty and racial income differences are complementary goals, but they are not identical. Poverty could be eliminated without eliminating racial economic inequalities. Racial income inequalities could be eliminated without eliminating poverty. If poverty were eliminated, the gap between black and white incomes would be reduced, since there are proportionally more blacks in poverty than whites, but it would not be eliminated. Similarly, eliminating racial income inequalities would reduce black poverty to the level of white poverty, but it would not eliminate either white or black poverty.

Thus, manpower programs need to be judged from two perspectives. How will they help eliminate poverty, and how will they help eliminate racial income inequalities? The present essay will emphasize their impact on racial income inequalities.

THE 1969 DISTRIBUTIONS OF INCOME

In 1969 the income of the medium black household was 60 percent of that of the median white household (see Table 3-1). While 18 percent of the white population had incomes above $15,000, only 6 percent of the black

Table 3-1. The 1969 Distribution of Income

Income Class (in thousands of dollars)	White (%)	Black (%)
0–1	2.8	6.3
1–3	12.0	22.2
3–5	11.2	19.0
5–7	11.9	16.2
7–10	20.0	17.5
10–15	24.3	12.7
15–25	14.3	5.5
25–50	3.1	0.5
50 & up	0.4	0.1
Median Income	$8,756	$5,291

Source: U.S., Department of Commerce, *Current Population Reports: Consumer Income, Household Income in 1969*, Series P-60, no. 72 (Washington, D.C.: Government Printing Office, 1970), p. 12.

population was similarly situated. At the other end of the distribution, 29 percent of the nation's blacks had incomes of less than $3,000, while only 15 percent of the whites were similarly situated.

Under the official definitions of poverty, the percentage of the population in poverty has fallen from 22.4 percent in 1959 to 12.2 percent in 1969. If the current rate were to continue, poverty would disappear in another ten years. Unfortunately, the conditional clause in the previous sentence is false. Those who can be helped by economic growth are rapidly leaving poverty, and, consequently, the proportion of families with no one in the labor force in poverty is rising rapidly. Basically, these families cannot be helped by either economic growth or manpower programs, but they now account for 35 percent of those in poverty. In addition, if a more plausible long-run definition of poverty, such as 50 percent of the median income (the approximate poverty standard when the official definitions were first adopted), is used, no progress has been made in eliminating poverty.

On the basis of relative income measures the economic inequalities between blacks and whites have changed little in the postwar period. When corrections for cyclical effects are made, the ratio of black to white incomes has not changed. Constant relative measures, however, imply widening absolute income differences. In 1947 the difference between white and nonwhite median family incomes was $2,302 (in 1967 dollars). By 1969 the difference had expanded to $3,208. The black income distribution seems to be following the same historical pattern as the white, but there is little evidence that the time lag between the two distributions is narrowing; blacks remain about thirty years behind whites.

Income distributions are actually the product of underlying distributions of human and physical capital, the level of productivity, the organization of the economic systems, discrimination, and many other factors. Unless positive evidence can be found that these elements are going to change autonomously, there is no reason to think that the income distributions will suddenly start to take new directions after 25 years of stability. New directions will depend on the quality and quantity of government programs designed to alter the income distributions; they are not inherent in the private economy.

THE CAUSES OF RACIAL INCOME DIFFERENCES

The gap between median black and white family incomes can be attributed to a variety of causes (see Table 3-2). This section will discuss these causes in terms of the point estimates of their quantitative importance, but the reader should remember that all of the estimates are subject to estimation error.

In high unemployment years when the national unemployment rate exceeds 6 percent, black incomes are approximately 50 percent of white incomes. Twenty percent of this difference (10 percentage points) can be attributed to poor macroeconomic policies and high unemployment. When unemployment is low (less than 3.5 percent nationally), black incomes rise to 60 percent of white incomes.

Another 4 percent of the difference (2 percentage points) can be attributed to the fact that black unemployment rates are approximately twice as high as white unemployment rates even when unemployment is low. Eliminating this part of the gap would require some structural program designed to equalize the burden of unemployment for blacks and whites.

Approximately 12 percent of the difference (6 percentage points) can be attributed to pure wage discrimination. Blacks are simply paid less for performing the same jobs as whites. Eliminating this part of the gap would require programs for eliminating wage discrimination.

Education and training each account for another 20 percent of the gap (10 percentage points). Equalizing education levels among blacks and whites would raise black incomes by 10 percentage points, and equalizing training levels among blacks and whites would raise black incomes by 10 percentage points. Education and on- and off-the-job training programs are necessary here.

The remaining 24 percent of the gap (12 percentage points) is attributable to occupational discrimination. Blacks are simply kept out of high-wage occupational categories to a greater extent than their lower educational attainment would warrant.

In a general sense all of the income differential can be attributed to discrimination. Blacks have less education than whites because of educational

Table 3-2. Causes of the Difference between Black and White Incomes

Cause	Percentage of Difference
Business Cycles (unemployment = 3.5% or less versus 6.0% or more)	20
Secular Unemployment Differentials	4
Pure Wage Discrimination	12
Less Education	20
Less Training	20
Occupational Discrimination or Barriers	24

Source: Lester C. Thurow, *Poverty and Discrimination* (Washington, D.C.: The Brookings Institution, 1969), chap. 3.

Note: Based on a high unemployment year when black incomes are 50 percent of white incomes.

discrimination; they have less training because of business and labor discrimination; and they have higher cyclical and secular unemployment than whites because of discrimination in job availability. From the programmatic vantage point, however, it makes sense to distinguish between those types of discrimination that *must* be eliminated with positive antidiscrimination policies, such as those run by the EEOC, and those types of discrimination which *can* be eliminated by remedial government programs of one kind or another.

Cyclical unemployment can be eliminated through better macroeconomic policies; education and training can be given in special programs. But differences in unemployment rates during periods of low unemployment, pure wage discrimination, and occupational barriers must be eliminated through direct enforcement of antidiscrimination laws. Together, these factors account for 40 percent of the income gap between blacks and whites. This leaves 20 percent of the task to macroeconomic factors and approximately 20 percent to education and 20 percent to training.

Although the different causes are enumerated separately in Table 3-2, it is imperative that they be viewed as a package and not as independent causes. Because of the complementarities among causes, it is not possible to achieve economic gains by affecting only one cause at a time. Less education is one of the causes of lower black incomes, but more education will not raise black incomes unless it is combined with complementary training programs, antidiscrimination programs to open job opportunities and equalize wage payments, and good macroeconomic programs to insure job availability. (The problem can be expressed in an algebraic manner by noting that the different causes are related to each other in a multiplicative manner rather than in an additive manner.)

Complementarities are the essence of eliminating racial income differentials. They mean that all of the factors which produce lower black incomes must be attacked simultaneously if noticeable improvements are to be made in the ratio of black to white incomes. If only one instrument is used, such as education, little improvement is apt to be noticed in black incomes. This is not to say that education is not valuable. It merely means that the returns to education are small unless education is combined with those training opportunities and jobs which make education valuable.

In a study of white and black male incomes in 1960, the combination of sixteen years of education plus thirty-five years of experience produced an income for whites that was 12 times as high as the effect of having the education alone and 6 times as high as the effect of having the experience alone. For blacks the respective numbers were 20 and 4. Education had a greater relative payoff, and experience had a lesser relative payoff. Absolute payoffs were much lower for blacks, however, for whites earned $8,155 and blacks only $4,856 if they had sixteen years of education and thirty-five years of experience.[1]

Serial attacks on the different factors which produce lower black incomes will have a limited effect on black incomes and will eventually pay off when enough of the problems have been attacked serially. It seems rather unrealistic, however, to expect blacks to hold still for education on the promise that eventually the training and antidiscrimination policies necessary to make education valuable will be forthcoming.

Let me be blunt. Manpower training programs without the other necessary ingredients such as effective antidiscrimination policies and tight labor markets are apt to be ineffective. The carrot of subsidized training programs will not work without the stick of antidiscrimination policies and tight labor markets.

THE STRATEGY OF MANPOWER PROGRAMS

The rhetoric surrounding manpower programs has viewed them primarily as methods for employing the unemployed. The reality of these programs differs from the rhetoric, but the rhetoric reflects the basis upon which the programs are conceived, organized, and justified. Unemployment is obviously important to particular individuals, but in aggregate it is not a major cause of lower black incomes. Only 4 percent of the income gap between whites and blacks can be explained by unemployment when the economy is operating at high levels of unemployment. This is true even among blacks who are in poverty. Only 6 percent of the black families in poverty have heads who are unemployed. The rest work, but some only part-time.

The basic problem among both blacks who are in poverty and those who are above poverty is one of upgrading. It is not a problem of finding an entry

[1] Lester C. Thurow, *Poverty and Discrimination* (Washington, D.C.: The Brookings Institution, 1969), p. 83.

job or a first job. Ghetto unemployment is important, but it should be held in perspective. It is not the major cause of either low black incomes or ghetto riots.

Quantitative importance is the major reason for emphasizing upgrading manpower programs, but there are several subsidiary factors that point in the same direction. Perhaps those individuals who subscribe to America's work ethic should be rewarded with manpower programs that are going to help them get ahead. If the system cannot or will not find ways to help those individuals who subscribe to the basic principles of the system, the system is probably not worth saving. There is also a question of costs and benefits. Most of the empirical evidence indicates that socialization, the work ethic, or industrial discipline (call it what you will) is the primary barrier to entry jobs, but it is exactly these qualities that are most difficult, if not impossible, to teach in manpower training programs. The absence of these qualities, rather than the absence of technical skills, is also what makes it difficult to merge manpower trainees with the regular labor force. Bad habits and low work standards drive out good habits and high work standards.

Some manpower programs, such as the Job Corps, have shown high benefit-cost ratios, but the low benefit-cost ratios found in many programs can be ascribed to problems of industrial discipline. Dropouts and absenteeism raise training costs and reduce benefits because workers are unable to hold onto their jobs – not because of lack of technical skills, but because of lack of industrial discipline.

By focusing on upgrading, the whole set of problems surrounding industrial discipline can be postponed, if not avoided. The individuals who are to be trained have demonstrated that they have industrial discipline by their employment record. They have problems, but not these problems. If there were no budget limitations in manpower training, the work ethic problem could not be avoided, but I would suggest that it be postponed, given the present circumstances of limited budgetary resources.

The previous arguments are arguments for a policy of creaming – start with the person who is easiest to aid and work down to the person who is most difficult to aid. Since our society has set the goal of eliminating poverty as well as racial income inequalities, the creaming should presumably start with the man who is easiest to move over the poverty line and work down to those who are most difficult to move over the poverty line. In this manner, manpower programs would have the greatest impact on both income redistribution goals.

Creaming has received a bad name, for it implies that those who are most in need are ignored. If society only had the instrument of manpower training programs to alter the income distribution, this would be true and might dictate against creaming. But society has other instruments. Manpower training programs are not a universal cure for every individual with a low income. Direct income redistribution has an important role to play.

The limitations of manpower training programs depend upon society's value judgments. These value judgments are important because it is not possible to judge manpower training programs simply in terms of economic costs and benefits. Both society and the individual being aided may prefer to have the individual earn his own income rather than simply be given an income. The value of this preference determines how far manpower training programs should be pushed as an instrument to eliminate poverty and racial income inequalities. Manpower training programs should be used whenever the economic benefits of training exceed the economic costs of training, but they should also be used as long as the value society places on earned income exceeds the net economic costs of training. Thus, if America places a $1,000 value on earned incomes as opposed to transfers, every training program in which costs are not more than $1,000 greater than benefits ought to be undertaken.

In our emphasis on the Puritan work ethic, Americans often talk as if every individual ought to be aided with manpower training programs, regardless of the costs. In other words, we place an infinite value on earned income versus unearned income. I doubt whether this is true, but if it is true, such a valuation ought to be clearly stated. In any case, no one can spell out the proper role for manpower training programs without a set of policy decisions on the premium to be placed on *earned* income. If cost minimization is the goal, income transfer programs will probably dominate training programs for all but the very young. Thus adult training programs need to be justified in terms of a premium to be placed on earned as opposed to unearned income. The dividing line between those to be helped by training programs and those to be helped by transfer programs will depend upon this premium. Without making the premium explicit, it will be impossible to plan efficient manpower training programs.

Those interested in manpower training programs ought to be the strongest advocates of direct income redistribution. Without such redistribution, manpower training programs will be politically forced to concentrate on those they are least likely to help. In the process, they will undoubtedly discover that benefits are often smaller than costs. Critics will point out the failures of the programs and call for their abolition. Direct income redistribution is a necessary ingredient for successful manpower training programs because it frees manpower training programs to do what they can do successfully.

Even when viewed as an income redistribution device, manpower training programs ought to "cream." They should begin with those who are easiest to help. This means those who are now working full-time, but who are still earning a low income. They have demonstrated the industrial discipline needed to succeed. In 1968 there were 4.6 million whites and 1.2 million blacks who worked full time and earned less than $3,000 per year. These should be the prime group for manpower training programs.

A MATTER OF TIME PREFERENCE

In *The Unheavenly City* Edward C. Banfield argues that programs to improve the skills and education of poor blacks fail because most poor blacks have high rates of time preference.[2] They are simply unwilling to sacrifice consumption today (invest) for the sake of more consumption tomorrow. As a result, they are unwilling to participate effectively in manpower training programs, since training inherently calls for current sacrifices for the sake of future benefits.

This argument needs to be clearly understood. If it is true, manpower training programs should be geared to blacks who are above the poverty line and have clearly demonstrated that they have reasonably low rates of time preference and are willing to make sacrifices. Manpower training should be used to close the income gap between blacks and whites at the upper end of the income distribution rather than at the lower end of the income distribution.

To be valid, the Banfield argument requires more than a demonstration that poor blacks have higher rates of time preference than those who are higher up the income scale. It requires a demonstration that the higher rates of time preference are determined by noneconomic factors (cultural or social) and not by economic factors.

Economic theory predicts that rates of time preference will differ among individuals and groups of individuals. An individual's current income level is one of the basic determinants of his rate of time preference. The smaller my current income, the higher its marginal utility and the less I can *rationally* afford to invest for tomorrow. I have a high rate of time preference, but an economically rational high rate of time preference. The man who is just on the margin of starvation today does not invest in increasing tomorrow's supply of food. To die today to have food for tomorrow is not a good economic investment. The rich can invest for tomorrow because they do not sacrifice much today.

To argue that blacks have higher rates of time preference than whites it is necessary to argue that blacks have higher rates of time preference than whites with the same incomes. Such an argument cannot be made, because the objective evidence points in the opposite direction. After correcting for current income levels, blacks tend to save more than whites with the same income.

[2] Edward C. Banfield, *The Unheavenly City* (Boston: Little, Brown & Co., 1968).

Operational rates of time preference include not only the individual's pure rate of interest but also an allowance for his risk or uncertainty premiums. The poor are less firmly established in society, have less information about labor markets, and are less certain that they will benefit from investment in human capital. For them, personal investment takes on aspects of a risky uncertain speculation. They rationally add a high uncertainty premium to an already high discount rate. The result is a further rational depression in the amount of human investment they are willing to undertake.

Finally, it is not at all obvious that the black who refuses to participate in educational or training programs or who drops out is being, ipso facto, irrational. The cost-benefit results from many programs are not encouraging, and there are, at the very least, enough failures to make entry into any program a risky investment.

To make manpower training programs work in this environment, actions must be taken to reduce individual rates of time preference and individual risk or uncertainty. Since rates of time preference can be reduced only by increasing personal incomes, enrollees in training programs must be paid good wages to increase their incomes. Risk and uncertainty can be reduced only by having definite jobs attached to the end of the training program. The route from *successfully* completing a training program to a good job (a high-income job) must be direct, visible, and without slippage. If this is to occur, workers must be of the best quality. Once again this points to a policy of creaming and maintaining reasonable quality standards in the training programs. Training for low-level jobs is a waste of time from the perspective of maintaining individual incentives.

INCENTIVES FOR FIRMS TO INVEST IN HUMAN CAPITAL[3]

Profit-maximizing firms and efficient public agencies require individuals with human capital. Skills, talents, and knowledge are necessary for both public and private production. Some of the necessary human capital may be acquired in the marketplace. Firms simply rent individuals who possess the desired human capital assets, just as they might rent physical capital. Individuals produce human capital assets because firms will rent them.

Some types of human capital assets, however, are difficult, if not impossible, to rent in the labor market. These assets are acquired through on-the-job training or experience. Firms create human capital because they are often the most efficient producers of human capital. Sometimes the employer has a monopoly on training capabilities. Only he possesses the equipment or en-

[3]For a more extensive discussion of investment incentives, see Lester C. Thurow, *Investment in Human Capital* (Belmont, Calif.: Wadsworth, 1970), chaps. 5, 6, and 7.

vironment in which the particular training can be given. Most production-line jobs fall into this category. The employer may also be a low-cost producer of training. He may be able to take advantage of economies of scale in training, or training may be a complementary product with production. Profits produced in the process of training may cover part or all of the costs of training, or they may exceed them. Individual work incentives may also be higher when training is provided on the job rather than in a school.

Firms find it profitable to increase the human capital of their labor forces because more human capital leads to more output. The profit-maximizing firm provides training until the marginal returns from training are equal to the marginal costs of training. If the marginal returns from training are greater than the marginal costs, more training is undertaken; if the reverse is true, less training is undertaken.

There are two sources of profit from training for firms. (1) Training increases labor's marginal product. If firms are able to appropriate some or all of the increase in labor's marginal product, profits can be earned from training. (2) If there are complementarities between physical capital and the quantity of human capital, increasing the quantity of human capital may lead to more returns to physical capital through more efficient utilization of physical capital.

Training can be general and specific. General training is useful to other firms in the economy, while specific training is useful only to the firm giving the training. In perfect labor markets all of the increases in labor's marginal product accrue to the individual in the case of general training and to the firm in the case of specific training. If increases in labor's marginal product were the only benefits to be gained from training, firms would pay for all specific training, but would not pay for general training. They might provide general training, but the individual would pay for it by accepting wages below his marginal product. Individuals, on the other hand, would never pay for specific training. They receive no benefits from it, for it is not salable in the labor market.

Given imperfect labor markets and monopoly powers, the beneficiaries of training and the investors in training are not so easily determined. A monopolistic employer may be able to appropriate gains from general training; a monopolistic union may be able to appropriate gains from specific training for its members. The investor may not be the beneficiary.

General and specific training are convenient analytic terms, but they actually represent two poles of a continuum. Few types of training are completely specific to one company, and little on-the-job training could really be considered completely general. Firms must decide how far they are going to move along the continuum between specific and general training; they cannot realistically choose to provide no general training and all specific training. In some isolated company towns, firms provide all training, including formal elementary and secondary education; in other situations firms provide almost no training of any kind.

In addition to appropriating part of labor's marginal product, firms may increase their profits from complementarities between human capital and physical capital. Just as the marginal product of labor depends on the quantity of physical capital with which it is combined in standard production functions, so does the marginal product of physical capital depend upon the quantity of human capital with which it is working. When the human capital of the labor force increases, the marginal product of capital rises. With a higher marginal product for capital, higher profits result.

Technically, a marginal increase in the quantity or quality of one factor does not affect the marginal product of another factor. In reality, however, such changes are never marginal in the technical sense. They are always larger. Thus, increasing the skills of the human labor force raises the returns to both physical capital and labor, not just to labor, because investing in human capital significantly alters the stock of labor with which capital works. The productivity of one asset depends upon the quantity of the other.

Complementarities between human capital and physical capital eliminate the sharp distinction between general and specific training. If training raises the marginal productivity of physical capital, firms can earn extra profits from training, regardless of whether training is general or specific. General and specific training may themselves be complementary. General training may be undertaken because it makes specific training more profitable. Thus the firm may be willing to pay for general training even when it cannot appropriate direct gains. It makes indirect gains from being able to appropriate increases in the returns to either physical capital or specific training.

Market imperfections may turn general training into specific training. Moving costs, pension plans, attachments to geographic areas and friends, seniority provisions, inadequate knowledge about alternative opportunities, and a host of other factors all lead to a higher probability that training returns can be appropriated by the investing firm. Institutional constraints may lead to firms investing in their employees' human capital. The existence of an internal labor market is one such constraint. If the labor market within a firm is separated from the external labor market by constraints on hiring, firing, or promotion, training labor cannot be hired from the external labor market, regardless of its availability.

While firms provide more training than they would in a simple world of general and specific training (almost no skills are really specific to just one firm), firms still have every incentive to hire the individual who requires the lowest training costs. This generally means the individual who has already acquired the most human capital. As a result the dispersion in human capital investments caused by differences in individual budget constraints (time preferences) is magnified by a firm's investment decisions. Either the stick or the carrot is necessary to offset such rational behavior. Firms must be forced to hire low-income workers or they must be bribed into hiring low-income workers.

Bribes, however, may not result in increased training activities. They may simply become subsidies for training activities that the firms would have undertaken in any case. Such "dead weight" losses are difficult to avoid, but simple efficiency demands an attempt to minimize them. This means that programs must be framed so that subsidies go to firms that hire workers they would not otherwise have hired or to firms that train and promote workers they would not otherwise have trained or promoted.

The only method for doing this is to establish a system of incentive payments (either grants or tax exemptions) where payments are made depending upon how much a firm is able to advance an individual's income. To avoid the problem of "dead weight" loss, the bonus or bribe should be based on how much the firm is able to advance an individual's income above what it would have been if his last year's income had advanced at the average rate in the economy. Thus, if an individual earned $2,000 last year and money wages rose 8 percent on the average, a firm would receive a grant or tax exemption depending upon how much the individual's income exceeded $2,160 in the current year. The bonus, however, may differ, depending upon the level of income as well as the increase in income. Thus an increase from $2,000 to $3,000 may be worth a larger grant or tax exemption than an increase from $3,000 to $4,000.[4]

With such a system the government is paying for the output it wants — relative income increases — and not for some inputs — training programs — that may, or may not, lead to the desired results. Administrative requirements are vastly reduced because the government need only monitor changes in income. (Such monitoring is already carried out by the Internal Revenue Services.) Governments do not need to monitor the quality of training programs. Firms with relative advantages in training abilities are allowed to concentrate on those individuals and income classes where they think they can increase incomes the most. If income increases can be caused by training workers with incomes above the level eligible for subsidies and then promoting lower-income workers into their positions, so much the better. Society does not want training *per se*. It wants relative income increases.

[4]The details of such a system have been worked out in Thurow, *Poverty and Discrimination*, p. 191.

CONSTRAINTS ON ALTERING THE RELATIVE DISTRIBUTION OF INCOME

Low unemployment (4.0 percent or less) is a necessary ingredient if manpower programs are to succeed in altering the distribution of income. In such years there is an excess demand for highly skilled and high-income workers. Low-income workers can be trained to fill such an excess demand. In years of high unemployment there is no excess demand for high-income labor. Workers can be trained and may even find good jobs, but in the process they simply bump another worker out of a job that he would have had. Given the queue nature of the labor market, such a step begins a process of downward bumping, or filtering, in which the worst worker in the queue eventually ends up unemployed with an income just as low as that previously enjoyed by the trained worker. The same process can be seen throughout the labor queue. Increasing the supply of college graduates means that they filter down into what had previously been the best high-school jobs. This lowers the average income of high-school graduates. The result is that a sharp difference is created between private returns and social returns. Privately the trainee may earn a good rate of return on the investment in his training, but socially the returns may be negative, for the system produces another low-income worker for every worker it helps out of a low-income status. Such a reshuffling of low-income workers may be desirable, but it does not solve the ultimate problem.

From an efficiency standpoint manpower training programs should be phased in and out of existence with the business cycle. During recessions, programs would be cut back or eliminated; during periods of expansion, programs would be started or expanded. Such cycles might have to be dampened to maintain the administrative capability of running programs at full employment levels, but this is the only argument for not eliminating manpower programs during recessions. From society's standpoint the programs cannot accomplish their objectives during a recession. No changes will occur in the distribution of income, because there is a fixed number and distribution of jobs.

Two types of relative income redistribution exist. In the first the distribution of income is altered without changing individual rank-order positions on the distribution spectrum; in the second the distribution of income is not altered, but individual rank-order positions on the distribution spectrum are altered. In theory the second type of income redistribution could occur during a recession. This would happen if a change were made in the extent to which laborers share low-income jobs and unemployment. Society might be more willing to tolerate a disperse distribution of income in a world where incomes were handed out on a lottery basis than it would be in a world where the same individuals always receive low incomes. From this perspective a manpower training program that resulted in the unemployment of an individual who had not previously suffered from unemployment would be deemed a success, even if the distribution of income did not change. Unfortunately the queue nature of the labor market means that unemployment quickly concentrates among those whose employment experience is similar to that of the trainee.

But why can programs not focus on changing the rank order of the labor queue. Theoretically such a reshuffling is possible, but both labor's and management's self-interest make such a reshuffling difficult to obtain. Those who are employed (the political majority in even the worst of depressions) have every incentive to fight to retain their jobs. Management wants rigidity in the labor queue for another reason. In an economy where informal methods of on-the-job training are the source of most labor skills, skills are passed from currently employed labor to new labor. They are not passed from management to new laborers. If laborers are to pass their skills along, they must have some assurance that newly trained workers will not take away their jobs. If such security did not exist, they would simply refuse to train new laborers. On-the-job manpower programs would come to an end if their objective was a reshuffling of unemployment. Trainees simply would not be trained. If every new economics student at MIT were a potential threat to my existence, I would simply stop teaching them economics or start teaching them false information. Most individuals, regardless of their current position in the labor queue, would do exactly the same. As a result manpower programs are devices properly reserved for periods of full employment. No job has ever been created by manpower training.

While it is possible to alter the distribution of income or individual positions on the distribution of income during periods of low unemployment, such policies will produce a *shortage* of low-wage workers. This will result in the elimination of certain occupations and industries, but it will also result in rapid wage increases in low-wage jobs and industries. If such jobs are in areas (the services, etc.) where productivity gains are not possible through better management, higher capital-labor ratios, or technical progress, the result will be increased inflationary pressures. These inflationary pressures may not be offset by decreased inflationary pressures in the areas of high-income jobs if labor shortages in these areas can be eliminated through productivity increases. In all likelihood successful manpower policies for altering the distribution of income will increase inflation.

DYNAMICS OF THE LABOR MARKET

All too often public policymakers view the labor market as an immutable vector of labor demands which must be accommodated by public policies designed to alter the vector of labor supplies. Round pegs are to be squared to fit into square holes. Fortunately the labor market does not operate in such a simple manner. The vectors of labor demands and supplies respond to each other. Sometimes the vector of labor demands changes to meet the vector of labor supplies and sometimes the vector of labor supplies changes to meet the vector of labor demands.

At the same time, however, the vector of labor demands serves as a rationing and selection device. As aggregate demand falls below the country's potential and unemployment rises, labor requirements rise as a device for ensuring each employer the best possible labor force. Workers from the top of the labor queue are always preferred to workers from the bottom of the queue. When they are not needed, workers at the bottom of the queue do not have the necessary qualifications for the job — i.e., someone else who is available has *relatively better* qualifications. Any employer who did not raise his entry and promotion qualifications in a recession would be acting irrationally. He would be failing to obtain the best possible labor force.

Worries about structural unemployment and automation are cyclical. Every recession and period of high unemployment since the Great Depression has produced analyses blaming high unemployment on structural unemployment. Yet the structural unemployment of the preceding recession always seems to vanish in the following boom. Groundless fears of the past do not prove that current fears are groundless, but there is not one shred of evidence that the change in unemployment rates between 1968 and 1970 can be explained by structural unemployment.

Given the adjustment process in the labor market, it is not possible to define the structurally unemployed as those people who are unemployed because their personal characteristics or skills are not adequate for employment. At any unemployment rate most of those who are involuntarily unemployed will have inadequate personal qualifications. Such inadequacies reflect the rationing process and not immutable labor demands.

As a result tight labor markets and full employment (an unemployment rate of between 3 and 4 percent) constitute the most effective governmental policies for income redistribution. Such policies automatically change many personal characteristics from inadequate to adequate. As a result, every 1 percent increase in the employment rate results in a reduction in the income differential between the twenty-fifth percentile of the population and the seventy-fifth percentile by 2½ percent.[5]

In the American economy low unemployment rates are associated with inflation. *Viewed simply as an income redistribution policy, such an association is good, not bad.* No one denies that inflation creates horizontal in-

[5] Lester C. Thurow, "Analyzing the American Income Distribution," *American Economic Review*, May 1970, p. 264.

equities (individuals with equal incomes in the absence of inflation will not have equal incomes in the presence of inflation), but *all of the evidence indicates that inflation is vertically equalizing.*[6] Income gaps between the top and bottom of the income distribution are reduced because the incomes of those at the lower end rise faster than those at the upper end. They benefit relatively more from expanding job opportunities and lengthening hours of work. During *full employment inflation* the wages of nonunionized low-income jobs tend to rise more rapidly than the wages of unionized jobs. As a result every 1 percent rise in the GNP deflator tends to reduce the income differential between the twenty-fifth percentile of the population and the seventy-fifth percentile of the population by 1 percent.[7]

Since there is no commonly accepted terminology for analyzing different types of unemployment in a dynamic labor market, let me suggest the following definitions. *Aggregate-demand unemployment* is unemployment that can be eliminated by expansionary fiscal and monetary policies without creating *more* inflation than policymakers are willing to tolerate. *Structural unemployment* is unemployment that could be eliminated through expansionary policies, but doing so would engender higher rates of inflation than policymakers are willing to tolerate. *Frictional unemployment* is unemployment that can be eliminated only through policies designed to change the structure of the labor market or the character of the individuals and jobs in that market. Such definitions have the advantage of focusing on the value judgements that are implicit in labor market analysis. Structural unemployment can increase if policymakers cease to tolerate as much inflation as they have in the past. Structural unemployment also depends on a weighing of the relative costs and benefits of both inflation and unemployment.

CONCLUSIONS

How can the two goals of income redistribution (altering the shape of the distribution of income and altering individual or racial positions upon the distribution of income) be accomplished? The evidence indicates that both goals can be accomplished, but the evidence also indicates that either goal would require sets of conditions that would be politically painful.

Full or overly employment would be needed to lessen the resistance to equal opportunity provisions and to altering the established distribution of earnings. The necessary employment levels would create substantial amounts of inflation. Unless offsetting changes were made to alter the Phillips curve, the American public would have to be willing to tolerate inflation in excess of

---

[6]*Ibid.*; Charles Metcalf, "The Size Distribution of Personal Income in an Econometric Model of the U.S." (MIT thesis), *American Economic Review*, September 1969.

[7]Thurow, "Analyzing the American Income Distribution."

5 percent per year if it were to have an unemployment rate of less than 4 percent.

Government incentive programs (such as the bonuses for increasing workers' incomes faster than the national average outlined above) would be needed to exert pressure on both the supply and demand sides of the labor market. Employers should be given an incentive to alter either the skills of their employees or the skills demanded in their jobs.

All of the evidence also indicates that the income positions of blacks and other minority groups cannot be altered by simply concentrating on their labor supply characteristics (education, training, etc.). Without vigorous and effective actions on the demand side of the market, changes in supply characteristics will not have much impact on minority incomes.

At the same time, the government would need to alter directly the demand for labor. There are two broad methods for altering specific labor demands. One method is to provide direct income transfers (family assistance plans, negative income taxes, etc.) that raise workers' reservation prices. Such plans reduce the supply of low-wage labor and place pressure on businesses to eliminate low-wage positions or go out of business. The second method is indirectly to alter the private wage structure. There are two possible techniques for the latter. Minimum wage laws can be used to specify lower bonds for wages, or public employment opportunities can be used to provide job opportunities at higher wage levels. In the second instance the opportunity of taking a public job forces private employers to adjust to public wage levels. In general this is the preferred technique because it avoids the adverse unemployment generated by higher minimum wages. At the same time, however, it should be realized that such wage pressure would make the U.S. Phillips curve more adverse than it already is.

Manpower programs, on either the demand or the supply side, have an important role to play in altering the distribution of income or individual positions upon the distribution of income, but they need other programs to create the necessary complementary conditions. Without these conditions manpower programs will not succeed in accomplishing either redistributional goal. If we are not willing to create the necessary complementary conditions, we should either abandon manpower programs or quit worrying when they do not work. There is no restructuring within manpower programs which can accomplish the postulated goals.

CHAPTER FOUR

MANPOWER PROGRAMS FOR A HEALTHIER ECONOMY

Sar A. Levitan

The sustained economic growth of the 1960s, with declining unemployment and only moderate inflation, generated a "new economics" based on the foundations of fiscal and monetary policies. The experience of the past decade seemed to confirm the doctrine of the Phillips curve that a little inflation could buy low unemployment, or vice versa. As the decade came to a close, however, the terms of trade were altered drastically. The Phillips curve, whatever its statistical validity, proved to be an undependable guide for action, as even substantial unemployment did not bring stable prices. Policy shapers had to choose according to their own values the most preferred combinations of unemployment and inflation. Although adequate to combat one problem at a time, the traditional tools were unable to fend off the dual foe, and thus spurred a search for additions to the government's arsenal. The aggressive use of manpower programs seemed to hold great promise.

THE ROLE OF MANPOWER POLICY

Some economists have argued that the difficult choice between unemployment and inflation can be eased by expanding the options available to policy planners. Manpower programs, they argue, have the potential to shift the trade-off to a more favorable position by changing the structure of the labor market, where inflationary pressures presumably originate.

The goals of manpower programs fall into three general categories: first, to help match the supply and demand for labor by increasing the efficiency of the labor market mechanism; second, to help workers who suffer particular disadvantages in competing for available jobs; and, finally, in the broadest sense, to provide every worker the vocational preparation needed for his chosen occupation, while insuring that society's labor requirements will be met.

During the 1960s the United States began to develop manpower policy as an added major tool in sustaining economic growth at stable prices and with minimum unemployment. Specific programs have been designed and implemented for each of the above goals. While politicians expanded the resources allocated to the development of manpower programs to help persons in need, it was also hoped that these efforts would improve the trade-off between unemployment and price changes, or, to use the technical terms of the economists, would shift the Phillips curve leftward, so that reductions in unemployment could be achieved with less pressure on prices.

Until the last decade federal manpower programs were reactions to specific crises, such as the emergency measures which were taken during the Great Depression and World War II. Measures that evolved during the 1960s may serve as the foundation for a comprehensive manpower policy that would, in turn, become part of overall governmental economic policy. Existing manpower programs can be divided into three categories: (1) labor market services to combat frictional unemployment by matching vacant jobs with idle but competent workers; (2) rehabilitation and training programs undertaken to reduce structural unemployment by preparing technologically displaced or disadvantaged workers for existing job vacancies and to promote upward mobility; and (3) public job creation to counteract cyclical and seasonal unemployment.

It may be safely assumed that some frictional unemployment will remain as long as workers are free to leave jobs or prepare for new employment and employers are free to lay off workers, relocate, or close their businesses. Structural unemployment also cannot be completely eliminated so long as changing technology continues to make some skills obsolete, so long as many entrants to the labor force are ill-prepared, and so long as the supply and demand for labor do not match perfectly. The manpower programs designed during the past decade were supposed not only to reduce the level of unemployment but also to help achieve stable prices.

CURRENT MANPOWER PROGRAMS

Federal outlays for manpower programs have risen more than thirteen fold during the past decade. In fiscal 1961 the federal government contributed less than $300 million to various manpower activities, half of which was allocated to the federal-state employment service network and the other half to vocational education and vocational rehabilitation. In fiscal 1972, $4.8 billion was spent in a broad array of efforts (Table 4-1). The countercyclical measures adopted in the summer of 1971 raised federal expenditures for manpower programs by $650 million during fiscal 1972. Clearly, manpower programs have been a growing industry, with a total enrollment at the end of 1971 of some 500,000 (Table 4-2). Though some of these programs obviously reduced unemployment by providing stipends and some work or training to participants, their effectiveness in shifting the Phillips curve leftward (easing inflation pressures) remains to be proven. Each program may have a different impact upon the trade-off, but only those efforts which affect persons already in the labor force, or persons expected imminently to enter, hold much hope of being useful as policy tools.

Table 4-1. Distribution of Federal Outlays for Manpower Programs,
Fiscal 1961 – 1972

Approach	1961 %	1964 %	1966 %	1968 %	1970 %	1972 % (estimate)
Institutional Training	1	17	30	26	22	18
On-the-Job Training	1	1	2	5	10	10
Work Experience and Work Support	9	6	25	27	22	35
Job Placement and Support	44	30	15	13	13	10
Administration, Research, and Support	3	4	5	5	6	5
Vocational Education	19	26	14	11	10	10
Vocational Rehabilitation	23	16	10	13	17	13
Total	100	100	100	100	100	100
Total Federal Outlays (millions)	$290	$607	$1,700	$2,403	$2,832	$4,764

Source: U.S., Office of Management and Budget.
Note: Percentages may not total 100 because of rounding.

Table 4-2. Enrollment in Manpower Programs, December 1971

Manpower Development and Training Act	
Institutional	53,123
On-the-Job	43,385
Neighborhood Youth Corps	
In-School and Summer	101,523
Out-of-School	38,693
Operation Mainstream	21,094
Public Service Careers	33,143
Concentrated Employment Program	32,660
Job Opportunities in the Business Sector	40,290
Work Incentive Program	111,582
Job Corps	22,116
Public Employment Program	83,224
Total	580,833

Source: U.S., Department of Labor, Manpower Administration.

Employment Services

Investment in job placement efforts increased more than threefold during the past decade, but the number of nonagricultural placements made by the public employment service declined almost continuously during the period, from 6.7 million to 4.6 million annually. At the same time, the total labor force was expanding at a rate of about 1.5 million jobs a year. One explanation for the declining number of employment service placements is the expansion of industries and occupations which do not usually turn to the public employment service for new employees. State and local governments, for example, normally utilize their own hiring channels and do not depend on public employment services. Another reason and one that has greater importance for the future, has been the emphasis placed upon serving the poor and the unskilled. Many employers may believe that the public employment service refers only marginal workers, and they therefore shun the public employment service or turn to it only to fill jobs that require the barest preparation.

Other activities of the employment service, however, promise increased potential for its placement activities as well as for a better unemployment-inflation trade-off. Efforts are underway to automate much of the public employment service. The most important activities in this area include:

1. A job-bank system for the accumulation and dissemination of current job-order information. Job orders submitted to the employment service in a labor market are microfilmed and distributed to public agencies that can effectively utilize this information in the placement process. Job banks now operate in forty-five states and cover over one-half of the labor force.

2. The conversion of the job banks into a computerized job-matching system. While the job bank is a relatively simple and inexpensive operation, the job-matching system involves sophisticated electronic hardware; and the matching of applicants with vacancies also requires difficult programming. The employment service is now experimenting with several computerized matching systems.

Efficient data handling does not create jobs. The computerization of the public employment service's activities will be of little help if employers do not turn to the local offices for job placement. The federal government departed in mid-1971 from a long-standing policy against compulsory registration by requiring employers under government contract to register job vacancies. Whether the effectiveness of the public employment service will be improved by this departure from voluntaryism remains to be seen.

The employment service is, however, more than just a placement agency. It also performs various services for both employers and job applicants. Until the mid-1960s, these were largely limited to the counseling and testing of applicants. The expanded responsibilities of the employment service required the local offices not only to reach out into communities to encourage unemployed and underemployed workers to apply for jobs but also to offer various services to applicants in order to enhance their employability. This may include the purchase of medical assistance, referral to training, or provision of other services. Most significant of these may be the provision of funds for child care, which frees mothers of preschool-age children to work. But, as long as the bulk of the public employment service's clientele remains unskilled and unemployed, a provision for their training is essential in order to place them in sustained employment.

Training

Effective training programs offer promise in reducing structural unemployment and inflationary pressures because skill improvement increases worker productivity and may also reduce the pressure on prices which results from labor bottlenecks. Helping those with the most severe labor market problems should also expand the supply of labor and in turn lower the pressure on wages so that there will be less of a price rise at any level of unemployment.

The impact of past manpower programs on the trade-off between unemployment and the rate of price change has not been measured; whether it ever will be is doubtful. Nor are conclusive data available about the extent to which the employability of trainees has been improved. A large proportion of total expenditures has been allocated to income maintenance (Table 4-3), and the long-run impact of actual training has not been ascertained. An attempt by the Labor Department to measure the changes in the earning capacity — and presumably the productivity — of former enrollees as compared with a control group has proven inconclusive, and the department has been slow in releasing the available data.

There was, until the 1970 recession, an increasing emphasis on private-sector participation through wider use of on-the-job training, subsidies to private employers, appeals to the corporate conscience, and government-business partnership programs. This approach gained its original impetus under the Johnson administration, but its continued and increased support stemmed from its compatibility with Republican ideals.

The benefits of private-sector participation are obvious. Where jobs are offered to disadvantaged workers without subsidy, the aims of manpower policy are achieved at little cost. To the degree that the business sector knows its own needs and is most skilled in preparing workers to meet these needs, the training it provides will be more efficient. With "hiring first and training later," jobs are assured to participants, and a built-in incentive to remain in training is created.

The Manpower Development and Training Act of 1962 (MDTA) provided for the reimbursement to employers of direct training costs. This involved a

Table 4-3. Functional Distribution of Manpower Funds in 1971

	OJT	Institu-tional	Work Support	Rehabili-tation	Job Placement Assistance
Remedial Education	1	14	3	1	*
Skill Training	15	30	2	6	*
Work Supervision	*	*	9	*	1
Health	*	1	*	18	*
Recruitment, Counseling, and Placement	3	7	5	28	82
Other Supportive Services	38	2	2	25	2
Program Administration	5	10	11	7	15
Allowances	38	36	68	15	*
Total	100	100	100	100	100
Total Federal Outlays (millions)	$159	$584	$429	$441	$460

Source: U.S., Office of Management and Budget.

*Less than 0.5%.

much lower outlay on the part of the government per trainee than did institutional training, but left to the employer the choice of trainees. Government officials found it difficult to ascertain whether the reimbursed training would have been done even without the government subsidy. To gain some control over the selection of new employees, if not over the training, the government changed the rules of the game and reimbursed employers for hiring and retaining only disadvantaged applicants. Apparently in an effort to overcome employer reluctance to hire employees certified by a governmental agency, the federal government also raised the ante paid to employers.

Job Opportunities in the Business Sector (JOBS) started off with much fanfare and apparently with a fair degree of success, though its achievements were usually exaggerated. Then, unfavorable economic conditions in 1970 and 1971 slowed expansion. JOBS funds that had been earmarked in anticipation of continued growth were re-allocated to other programs because of the meager participation of employers.

In the early days of the JOBS programs, costs per hire were almost $3,000, nearly twice as high as costs under MDTA-OJT. This increase was necessary in part because the JOBS clientele was more disadvantaged. However, some of the increase was unrelated to employers' actual training costs and was instead an inducement for hiring.

Little is known about the training offered under JOBS, but fragmentary evidence suggests that in many cases it is little more than what is normally offered. Many of the disadvantaged hired under JOBS would likely have been placed in similar slots even without subsidies. These subsidies were not sufficient during 1970 and 1971 to induce hiring in the face of a recession, so the program was refocused, with less emphasis being placed on the disadvantaged.

If training has paid off in shifting the Phillips curve, the impact should be most pronounced in youth programs. The training programs most clearly designed for youth have been the Job Corps and, to a lesser extent, the skill centers under the Manpower Development and Training Act. The Job Corps was launched under the Economic Opportunity Act of 1964 to provide vocational and basic education to youths in a residential setting, under the assumption that removal from debilitating home environments would be necessary for training to be effective. Two types of centers were made available for men in the initial years of the program. Those most deficient in preparation for work were placed in rural centers, where the emphasis was on basic education combined with conservation work; those with better education received intensive vocational training in urban centers. For women, centers were opened in smaller urban areas; these emphasized training for clerical and service positions and had fewer educational offerings, since women, as a rule, had more schooling than men.

Coming into office with the promise to end the waste in the Job Corps, the Nixon administration did more than trim the fat off the program; it closed 59 of 123 centers. Although a careful procedure was set up to insure that the least-effective centers were closed and a variety of performance factors were considered and then weighted, enrollments in urban centers were cut most drastically, though their performance was relatively better than that of rural centers. Careful analysis of the postenrollment experience of Job Corps men and women revealed improvements in employment and earnings, but it was not clear whether these justified the very high costs of training.

The Neighborhood Youth Corps (NYC) was designed as a work experience, income maintenance, and training program for youths. There are three types of operations. Part-time jobs are provided for those in school, under the assumption that extra income will forestall dropping out for economic reasons. The summer NYC employs youths who might otherwise be "on the streets," the aim being to cushion their return to school the next fall. For out-of-school youths, NYC provides jobs and training, but, most of all, income, during the years of least employability. NYC has remained largely an income maintenance program, offering little training or preparation for work.

MDTA skill centers offer training for a number of alternative occupations, counselors to help with occupational choice and personal problems, and a prevocational orientation period to acquaint the trainee with various occupational options before he or she chooses one. Training modules, occupational clusters, and training "ladders" are combined to provide a number of broad skill areas in which trainees can find the specific occupations that best suit them. Flexibility is also attained by allowing students to enter at frequent intervals and leave when they reach their training goal.

A major concern of skill center administrators is that, over time, these centers have tended to become segregated institutions for the disadvantaged. However, a new thrust – integrating MDTA skill centers into community colleges – allows greater prestige, a mingling of disadvantaged and regular students, and a broader selection of occupation, which might motivate trainees to continue in regular enrollment.

Conceptually, the most anti-inflationary manpower program has been the drive to convert relief recipients – most of whom are not employed – into productive workers and taxpayers. President Kennedy described the effort as "rehabilitation not relief"; President Nixon has used the slogan "workfare instead of welfare." Thus far, manpower authorities have been largely frustrated in designing effective programs which would improve the employability of relief recipients. Among the several public assistance programs, attention has been focused on Aid to Families with Dependent Children (AFDC), whose ranks have been swelling continuously since the end of World War II and particularly during the past decade.

Despite the decline in poverty and unemployment brought by sustained economic growth during the 1960s, and despite a variety of other rising expenditures in aid of the poor, AFDC has grown steadily. Having about doubled during each decade from 1936 to 1966, AFDC again doubled within four years. By mid-1971 more than 10 million persons were on AFDC rolls. A number of contributory factors can be identified, but the relative ease of qualifying and the increased attractiveness of AFDC as an income source have played paramount roles in the expansion of AFDC. Cash payments during the 1960s increased about 50 percent faster than did the spendable earnings of workers with families. In addition, the value of in-kind benefits, such as food stamps, Medicaid, and public housing, increased even faster.

Programs were initiated under the 1964 antipoverty legislation and under the 1967 social security amendments to place employable adults on relief in training or jobs. These efforts have not worked well, however, and, at President Nixon's prodding, Congress is now in the process of overhauling the public assistance system. These reform efforts run into the thorny problems of providing adequately for those who cannot work, maintaining incentives for the able-bodied to contribute to their own support, and keeping costs at a level which is acceptable to the majority that foots the bill.

Any action Congress takes on President Nixon's proposals to induce or coerce public assistance recipients to enter gainful employment is likely to have little effect on shifting the Phillips curve in the desirable direction. Moreover, the initial costs would be considerable; the bill approved by the House carried an initial annual price tag which was about $5 billion above current welfare expenditures. Since most AFDC family heads are females with small children, the government may have to provide child care facilities in order to free many mothers for work. According to HEW estimates, the annual cost for all-day care for preschoolers is some $1,800; for children attending school, it is about a third as much. For a mother with one pre-school-age child and one school-age child, the annual cost for day care could amount to $2,400. Another $1,000 might be added for the initial cost of training. The Labor Department has estimated that, largely because of the high dropout rate, governmental outlays to place a mother in a job amount to over $5,000, in addition to public assistance payments. But, even then, the mother's earnings would have to be considerably above the average amount earned by females with limited skills and education before she could become economically independent. There may be persuasive reasons to encourage the economic independence of mothers and to induce them to choose work over relief, but the desire to avert inflationary pressures is not one of them.

Another hope for public training has been that the acquisition of new skills would improve the productivity of the work force and eliminate bottle-necks. Government subsidies were expected to induce employers to upgrade their labor force and, in the process, open up new jobs at the entry level for unskilled workers. While the Johnson administration favored direct subsidies to employers, others have proposed that tax incentives be offered to em-ployers to cover training costs. The latter notion was popular with most Republicans in the Ninetieth Congress who endorsed the Human Investment Act, which proposed a 10 percent tax cut for wages paid to trainees in order to reimburse employers for training nonmanagerial or nonprofessional em-ployees.

The major appeal of the tax incentive lies in the belief that the inducement will eliminate bureaucratic meddling in private business while it encourages business to pursue socially desirable goals. It is not clear, however, whether the sought-after goals can be achieved without government intervention. In the absence of governmental monitoring, business would do what comes naturally — hire the most acceptable workers and provide the same training to employees as it had in the past. Though President Nixon appeared to favor the Human Investment Act approach, he has not formally proposed it, and the notion has not received careful consideration in Congress.

The idea of using federal funds for upgrading, either through tax incentives or direct subsidies, remains the subject of much rhetoric but of little action. Given the limited resources available for manpower programs and the increas-ing emphasis upon helping the poor and the disadvantaged, very few resources are left to lesser priorities, and upgrading has never received top billing on the manpower agenda. The limited activity reflects also not only inadequate fore-sight about future manpower needs but, more significantly, the result of controls exercised by vested interests over entry and training in certain oc-cupations. The current glut of engineers and assorted Ph.D.'s in science is an illustration of the former, and shortage of health personnel is a manifestation of the latter.

Job Creation and Countercyclical Efforts

The use of manpower outlays as a countercyclical measure, an outgrowth of the 1970 recession, is the latest weapon in the ever-expanding arsenal of manpower policy. These countercyclical mechanisms, however, reflected the ambivalence of the administration and Congress about the tolerable level of unemployment. In connection with releasing added manpower funds during periods of high unemployment, the administration proposed that a trigger mechanism become operative when the total national unemployment rate averaged 4.5 percent during three consecutive months; but, in connection with the automatic extension of unemployment insurance during the recession, the law provided that the mechanism become operative when *covered* unemployment reached 4.5 percent, or when total unemployment reached 5.6 or 5.7 percent.

While the extension of the duration of unemployment insurance payments may be an effective counter-cyclical measure, President Nixon's proposal to expand manpower funds during a recession was modest indeed. The president proposed that manpower funds be expanded by 10 percent when the trigger mechanism became operative. Since less than $2 billion in manpower funds were covered by the proposal, the 10 percent boost would have raised annual manpower outlays during the recession by $200 million at most. The administration proposed that these funds be allocated for training workers for jobs that might be expanded when recovery occurs.

The use of public employment as a countercyclical strategy, with permanent or temporary expansion during periods of economic decline, was the intent behind the Emergency Employment Act (EEA). Signed into law in July 1971 to combat the recession, it authorized outlays of $1 billion in fiscal 1972 and $1.25 in fiscal 1973 for the creation of an estimated 130,000 jobs in the public sector. The EEA was implemented very rapidly with the intent of getting people on the job as quickly as possible. Monies were distributed among states and cities or counties with populations over 75,000. To assure the quickest possible implementation, federal regulations were kept to a minimum, with maximum authority and responsibility for the program being left to state and local officials. The jobs were reserved for the unemployed or underemployed, and they were explicitly transitional in nature; funding would be geared to the aggregate unemployment rate, and half of the EEA participants would eventually be moved onto permanent payrolls.

Contrary to conventional wisdom about the snail's pace of governmental activity, the EEA experience showed that manpower programs can serve as an effective tool to counteract a recession, though not necessarily as a counter-cyclical tool. Within four months of the first allocation of EEA funds, 79,000 persons were reported to be on the job. Nine-tenths of these had been unemployed for at least a week, so the program had some impact on unemployment. A variety of jobs were filled, and most appeared to be fairly productive, as firemen, policemen, clerks, and typists were hired.

The EEA experience demonstrated some of the inherent problems in using public employment as a countercyclical strategy. The major problem was one of scale. Despite the fact that the EEA was the largest single manpower program, it provided jobs for less than 3 percent of the unemployed by the end of 1971 and a much smaller proportion of the total number inside and outside of the labor force who had been hurt by the recession. It may have been possible to double or even triple the EEA appropriations and to distribute the funds with some semblance of order; but the massive commitment of resources needed to make a noticeable dent in unemployment would have been impossible, at least within the time constraints needed to make the effort worthwhile as a countercyclical weapon. Hiring 130,000 persons in six months was a notable achievement, but the bulk of these persons were not on the job until the end of this period. Since the recession had been in full swing for at least a year before congressional action was taken, and another four months were needed to get a majority of potential participants on the job, the program reached its full scale as recovery began.

A final problem is that, despite claims to the contrary, countercyclical public employment is a one-way street — state and local jobs can be expanded, but contraction may be more difficult and painful. For instance, under the EEA, the states and localities were informed that one-half of all participants must be moved into permanent jobs upon the expiration of EEA support. But this was no guarantee that the states and localities could absorb employees hired with EEA funds. Thus, pressure began to be exerted by mayors and governors to change EEA from a transitional to a permanent program, and this may well be in the cards. While there may be good reason for expanding the public sector, EEA might even contribute to inflationary pressures when recovery is achieved.

Though experience with the Emergency Employment Act demonstrated that a public employment program can be implemented rapidly and is worthwhile during a recession, it has not shown that it can be a major countercyclical tool. Funds used to hire the unemployed are probably more directly effective than other forms of public expenditure, but public employment policies cannot be implemented on a sufficient scale or with sufficient flexibility and timeliness to entitle them to parity with other forms of policy designed to expand overall demand.

In expanding federal funds allocated to job creation in the public sector under the EEA of 1971, Congress may have been motivated by other than theoretical economic considerations; but it would appear that the congressional action reflected little faith in utilizing manpower programs as part of a countercyclical policy. Many economists would no doubt agree. If manpower programs are to be utilized as a countercyclical device, it must be reasonably anticipated that the faucets will be turned on and off at will in accordance with the dictates of economic needs. Experience, however, has shown that this is not a reasonable expectation. It takes considerable time to expand manpower programs: training facilities have to be organized and personnel assembled; courses have to be developed; and trainees have to be selected and enrolled. And the training of individuals cannot be terminated abruptly because average unemployment drops below a certain predetermined level.

Nonetheless, since every little bit helps, it would be a mistake to use the limitations of manpower programs as an argument against utilizing them as a countercyclical measure. If President Nixon's proposal appeared too modest, Congress could have extended the trigger mechanism by granting an additional boost in manpower funds for step increases in unemployment above 4.5 percent. For example, if manpower funds had been boosted by 10 percent for each 0.2 percent increase (above 4.5 percent) in unemployment over a period of three months, there would have been a 60 percent automatic increase of manpower funds by mid-1971. There should be little concern that the need for additional funds would suddenly disappear. Experience has shown that unemployment is slow to drop during a period of recovery, and the additional training funds could be well utilized to prepare workers for expanding jobs. Moreover, unlike fiscal and monetary policies, manpower expenditures are directed at those most in need of help. Dollar for dollar, manpower programs probably have a greater impact on unemployment than do other types of spending; expanding them may be the best way to help the unemployed when demand slackens.

Little congressional effort has been made thus far to counteract seasonal unemployment. This lack of action may be explained by the wide diversity in climate and economic conditions in the various regions of the country, which seriously obstructs the development of federal policy. But other industrial countries, particularly Germany and Canada, have adopted various incentives intended to counteract seasonal unemployment. The most significant U.S. manpower program to counteract seasonal unemployment is the annual expansion of the Neighborhood Youth Corps, which provides income, if little employment, to as many as half a million unemployed youths who are out of school during the summer.

THE LIMITATIONS OF MANPOWER POLICY

Although ample room remains for further expanding manpower programs, it is doubtful that the phenomenal growth which was experienced during the past decade can be duplicated, nor is it even clear that it should. Manpower efforts are likely to remain a junior partner in the formulation of economic policy. Given the present magnitude of manpower programs, their limitations in affecting economic policy become obvious. The tax cut of 1964 pumped some $14 billion annually into the economy. The 1968 surtax provided only somewhat more than half of that amount, but this is still three times the annual outlays for manpower programs. Moreover, as noted, unlike monetary and fiscal policies, manpower programs cannot be expanded or contracted easily.

Nonetheless, there has been no lack of advocates of expanding manpower programs. Most of these advocates, however, fail to recognize the problems of administering manpower programs, overcoming reluctance by vested interests, and assessing prospective manpower needs. Even if we were to make the heroic assumption that these obstacles could be overcome, the case for continued expansion of manpower programs as an economic rather than as a social or welfare tool would still remain to be proved. The inherent obstacles to adopting manpower programs as countercyclical tools are formidable. None of the recessions since the end of World War II has thus far lasted more than thirteen months, and most skill shortages also have been of short duration. With start-up time, recruitment and screening of candidates and instructors, actual training time, and allowances for those who will not complete training, the time period between recognition of a particular shortage and delivery of the first candidates may stretch into years. Some training efforts under existing programs, launched in a period of immense need, have provided graduates only after the need was long past. Advocates of expanded budget continue to hope that manpower forecasting will be improved. Greater investment in early warning systems would provide better insight into projected manpower needs. But, until these anticipations are realized, the constraints on expanding manpower programs will remain very real. It would take much more to overcome discrimination in hiring and in the control exercised by special interest groups over entry and training.

Any program which enhances the employability of marginal workers, reduces labor market frictions, expands the supply of skills, or reduces institutional barriers to employment makes possible lower unemployment or reduced wage costs per unit of output. It does not follow, however, that the inflation-unemployment trade-off will necessarily be improved. The additional supply of labor which results from training may actually raise unemployment, and the cost of training may raise total costs even though direct unit labor costs may decrease. In the short run, the resources allocated to training may actually reduce the total labor supply engaged in production because skilled labor would be assigned to training.

The extent to which trainees fill jobs that would otherwise have remained unfilled or that would merely have displaced other workers is also crucial, though practically unresolvable. Displacement is frequently justified as an attempt to "spread the burden" of unemployment beyond those on the bottom of the economic pile. While this may be desirable on equity grounds, it actually detracts from efficiency by spending money while gaining no net yield.

Moreover, tradition and powerful institutions tend to determine wage rates and prevent sharp improvements in the unemployment-inflation trade-off. In addition, inflationary pressures may, but do not necessarily, originate in the labor market. In the early 1960s, for example, price increases were considerably larger than unit labor-cost boosts, and therefore reflected large increases in nonlabor costs. Devices other than manpower programs are needed to alter the observed relationship between prices and unemployment.

LOOKING AHEAD

This brief review of manpower programs also suggests that the presumed salutary effect of shifting the Phillips curve is more an article of faith than an established fact. The delivery of manpower services, the training of the unemployed and the underemployed, and the upgrading of employed workers should be judged on their own merits and not by their impact upon aggregate economic activity. If manpower programs ease the unemployment-inflation trade-off, so much the better. The controlling factor for the expansion or contraction of manpower efforts should be the needs of individuals and not an abstract, presumed trade-off. Some improvement in the unemployment-inflation trade-off may be anticipated from specific job training and placement programs. But these expectations do not by themselves justify further expansion of manpower programs, for current efforts do not warrant inflated notions about the impact of manpower programs.

The effectiveness and role of manpower programs should be neither exaggerated nor denigrated. Experience has shown that the employment stability and earnings of many manpower program participants have improved. Other participants have not gained, primarily because manpower programs were being asked to solve social and economic problems beyond their reach. Skill training is no substitute for adequate economic growth or job creation, and improvements in labor market operations do not create jobs. Manpower policies can hardly instill a preference for work over welfare, nor can they single-handedly overcome the cumulative disadvantages of discrimination, which are usually the cause of low earnings.

The relatively short experience with manpower programs during the 1960s must be viewed as experimental; hence, the heretofore limited success of these tools does not preclude reliance on them in the future. From the many trials and failures experienced during the past decade, lessons were learned, services were improved, and new options were provided to disadvantaged persons, especially blacks, to improve their abilities and thus gain entry into the mainstream economy. In many cases, manpower programs offer a second chance to those who failed in, or were failed by, the educational system and for those whose skills have been eroded by technological change. As more knowledge is gained about the needs of particular individuals and about the effectiveness of particular services or a combination of services in meeting these needs, the manpower programs may become an alternative for those who do not succeed in the regular school system. The experience gained from the manpower programs may also help the regular school system to avoid past mistakes.

Experience has shown that in the short run the unemployment rate can be lowered or raised almost at public will. The problem is to achieve sustained high employment without undue inflation, and the key issue, therefore, is the trade-off between unemployment and inflation. Despite the rhetoric of politicians and economists, it is not likely that we can achieve in the immediate future both high employment and stable prices. Given this dilemma, experience dictates measures that will cushion the negative effects of inflation in order to sustain a high-employment economy. The progress made during the past three or four decades justifies some optimism that increasingly sophisticated designs will ease the choice between inflation and unemployment. Meanwhile, we must make the hard decisions between the two, and that remains a matter of personal values.

CHAPTER FIVE

THE OVERALL IMPACT OF AN ACTIVE LABOR MARKET POLICY IN SWEDEN

Rudolf Meidner and Rolf Andersson

THE AIM OF ECONOMIC POLICY

A superficial look does not disclose any decisive difference between the aim of economic policy in Sweden and that in other highly developed industrial societies. The main goals are full employment, economic stability, a high rate of growth, and greater equality in the distribution of income. In principle it should be possible to quantify the first two objectives and to make them operational as targets for economic policy — e.g., a level of unemployment or a rate of price increase which may not be exceeded without causing an immediate counteraction. Harder to fix are the latter two objectives: the "highest possible" growth of Gross National Product (or of overall welfare as expressed in terms other than GNP), and a more even income distribution, when an exact description of the structure of incomes pursued is lacking.

The following discussion will deal primarily with the compatibility of the first two goals mentioned and with the role imparted in Sweden to labor market policy as a means to ease this compatibility. Economic growth and income distribution will be referred to only insofar as labor market policy, used as a stabilizer, also affects those objectives. This limitation does not imply a downgrading of growth and income objectives as such, or a disbelief in the potential of labor market policy to further these aims *directly* and with other measures. The limited scope is imposed entirely by the necessity to concentrate on the part of economic policy which is particular to Sweden:

This article was originally prepared at the beginning of 1971, before a severe recession hit Sweden. The authors are grateful to Mrs. Lucienne Forsse for research assistance.

the use of selective labor market policy as a means to overcome the classical conflict between high employment and price stability.

A closer study of authoritative statements, however, shows that the Swedish government has given higher priority to full employment while, in its yearly opening statements to the Riksdag, tending to push price stabilization into the background.[1] As a matter of fact, the level of ambition concerning the meaning of the concept "full employment" has risen steadily during the postwar period, while the claim for price stability has grown weaker. This does not imply that the full employment–price stability dilemma has been solved to the advantage of the full employment goal; rather, the dilemma has acquired a new dimension through a continuous redefinition of the full employment goal.

As a result of the rising ambition regarding what is meant by "full, productive, and freely chosen employment," registered unemployment has gradually lost value as an indicator of changes in the level of employment. It is no longer considered that "full employment" has been achieved when current unemployment can be explained entirely by unavoidable unemployment of short duration in connection with a change of employment (frictional unemployment) and by a residual group of "unemployables." Labor market policy has grown more and more qualitative and, as such, has brought new groups into the labor force, groups previously excluded on social, institutional, or other grounds.

The concept of unemployment used in labor force surveys, which includes also latent unemployment,[2] meets the higher level of ambition and gives a better picture of the actual situation on the labor market than does the employment service's register of unemployed. Not even this extended measure of unemployment, however, indicates changes in demand level which lead to shifts from groups in the labor force to groups outside the labor force. These can be measured by fluctuations in the rate of participation, but are not easily interpreted, for they are influenced by changing trends connected with, among other things, educational expansion, a lower retirement age, urbanization, structural changes in industry, institutional changes which facilitate gainful employment for married women, etc.

In conclusion, there seems to be no clear operational yardstick for measuring unemployment or employment which corresponds to the level of ambi-

[1] See, for instance, the statement made by the minister of finance at the opening of the Riksdag in January 1971: "The main objectives of economic policy in 1971 are evident: full employment, continued high rate of growth, a more even distribution of income, and better regional balance. *To this must be added* the need to stabilize the level of prices" (annex 1 to Sweden's 1971 Finance Bill, *budget statement*, p. 12; italics added).

[2] Persons who stated that they would have sought employment during the week of the survey had they thought they could get a suitable job in the neighborhood.

tion of economic policy as regards full employment. Registered unemployment can best be compared to that part of the iceberg (of the idle potential of manpower) which is visible above the surface. With an employment objective as ambitious as Sweden's is by international comparison, an objective which can be realized primarily by means of an extensive manpower policy, the dilemma between high employment and stable money value can be expected to be particularly acute in Sweden.

The aim as regards price stability has developed the opposite way – i.e., ambitions have gradually been reduced. Since the days of Knut Wicksell,[3] there has been a strong tradition in Sweden to look upon price stability as the reflection of balance in the economy. Erik Lindahl[4] defended the theory that the level of prices should vary in inverse proportion to productivity for economic balance to be maintained. By the mid-forties, traces of that line of thought could still be found in public government statements, though with the qualification that the rise in prices caused by shortages during the war were tolerable. During the postwar period and on into the fifties, the periodically inflationary price increase was seen, still in the Wicksellian spirit, as the result of a demand gap, and a great deal of intellectual effort was devoted to quantifying the extent of this gap. The illusion that the value of money could be stabilized by eliminating excess demand through general measures stood out clearly in most government statements during that time.

Not until the late fifties were attempts made to analyze cost inflation. In the process, economic balance was found to be a prerequisite, but far from satisfying, condition for price stability in a thoroughly organized society like Sweden: varying productivity conditions, rigid price determination (particularly downward), income ties, and labor organizations' efforts to obtain compensation for changed wage relations initiate and maintain a process of price increase which can be subdued but not stopped by restrictive policy.[5] The idea was further developed, in close relation to the multisector model tested by the Norwegian Aukrust,[6] by three economists from labor and management organizations who tried to analyze the development of productivity and of prices in the sector of the Swedish economy which is exposed to competition, as well as in the sheltered sector.[7]

[3] Knut Wicksell, *Interest and Prices* (London, 1936).

[4] Erik Lindahl, *Studies in the Theory of Money and Capital* (London, 1939).

[5] These ideas were first developed extensively in the report of a committee for which representatives from all larger political parties and labor organizations were responsible: *Mål och medel i stabiliseringspolitiken*, [Ends and Means of a Stabilization Policy] (Stockholm, 1961).

[6] O. Aukrust, F. Holte, and G. Stolz, *Instilling fra Utredningsutvalget for intektsoppgjörene, 1966* [Report from the Committee on Wage Agreements, 1966] (Oslo, 1966).

[7] G. Edgren, K.-O. Faxén, and C.-E. Odhner, "Wages, Growth, and the Distribution of Income," *Swedish Journal of Economics*, September, 1969.

The authors' conclusions are, in short, that a country whose economy to a great extent depends on international trade and whose labor organizations are powerful must accept some continuous rise in prices, unless it operates with successive changes in the rate of exchange.[8] This deviation from traditional Swedish price stabilization objectives was expressed most authoritatively in a statement by the minister of finance in 1965: "A moderate rise in prices by 2 to 3 percent a year during a period of boom appears to be unavoidable if we give as high a priority to full employment as we do now and shall so continue to."[9]

In summary, against the background of the modifications described above, the main objectives of economic policy can be formulated as follows: striving for a level of employment which satisfies the wishes of the citizens as regards employment (whether or not they are in the labor force and whether or not their marginal productive input corresponds to the market wage) *and*, at the same time, for a rate of price increase that does not exceed the rise in costs which derives from foreign influence but which spreads to the entire economy through the mechanism of wage determination. This objective constitutes a deviation from the traditional concept of full employment, based on a market equilibrium between actual (not potential) supply of, and demand for, labor, and from the claim for economic balance which has price stability as its chief criterion. Postwar experience has shown that even this more sophisticated combination of objectives creates a severe dilemma for economic policy.

Before turning to the discussion of a model for economic policy which could possibly solve this dilemma, we shall summarily touch upon two other objectives that are central features of economic policy but that are peripheral in this context: economic growth and income distribution. Our theory is that labor market policy is the core of the stabilization model to be described later (see pp. 123-25). Labor market policy can play a role in relation to economic growth and a more even distribution of income, but, compared to other, direct measures, this role is secondary.

A high rate of growth is operationally synonymous with the rapid growth of the GNP. In the Swedish debate the question has been raised, in the same fashion as elsewhere, whether GNP adequately reflects welfare growth.[10] The frailty and shortcomings of GNP calculations in this respect are evident. But, even when we limit GNP as a measure of welfare — and thus neglect the

---

[8] "The rise in prices derives from rises abroad, from the market mechanism, and from strivings for equality in income" (*ibid.*, p. 154).

[9] Gunnar Sträng, "Är inflationen oundviklig?" [Is Inflation Unavoidable?], *Svensk Sparbankstidskrift*, 1965, no. 2-3, p. 72.

[10] E. J. Mishan, *The Costs of Economic Growth* (London, 1967).

welfare-raising effects in the Pareto-optimizing sense of increased and qualitatively improved employment opportunities for unemployed and underemployed persons — it seems that a larger input of selective labor market measures stimulates welfare growth. Some economists have presented the theory that a rising level of employment may retard productivity growth if manpower with low marginal productivity joins the labor market.[11] A cost-benefit analysis from the point of view of society at large, including the reduction of nursing costs, the activation and rehabilitation effects of work, etc. (added as welfare function to Ohlin's figure), is likely to give a positive balance far beyond the level of employment which corresponds to the maximum (position *II*) (e.g., 95 percent) in Ohlin's production function.

However, of greater importance to growth than the aforementioned effects is the fact that selective labor market policy facilitates structural change in

[11]B. Ohlin, *The Problem of Employment Stabilization* (New York, 1949). Ohlin illustrates the relationship with the figure below, in which productivity reaches a maximum at employment level *I* and the production function has its maximum at employment level *II*. To the right of position *II*, "overfull employment" prevails, in Ohlin's terminology.

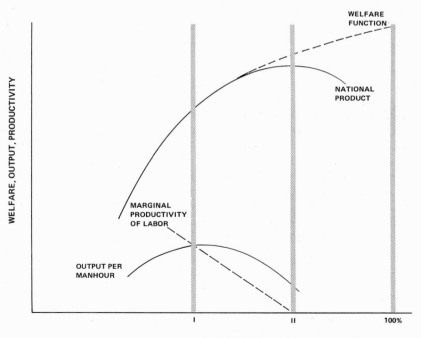

the economy and the removal of manpower from low-productive to high-productive and expanding firms and industries. The pace of this process of change, whose mainsprings are urbanization and concentration tendencies, is ultimately set by the resources labor market policy has at its disposal to ease adjustment and, as far as possible, to compensate for the costs and individual welfare losses engendered in the wake of adjustment.

A more even distribution of income is a goal to be reached primarily by way of wages, fiscal, and social policies. But even an intensified employment policy can make a valuable contribution to income leveling. The first report[12] delivered by the Commission of Inquiry into Low Income Groups clearly bears out that the effects of differences in wages are reinforced by differences in total work time per year. This is a question not only of actual unemployment but also of various forms of underemployment.

Hence we conclude that no real conflict can be said to exist between Sweden's employment objective, on the one hand, and her growth and distribution objectives, on the other. Nor is there anything in the postwar development of the Swedish economy to show that a high and increasing level of employment would have had a retarding effect on the rate of economic growth, which has been faster in Sweden than the average for OECD countries. Statistics to support international comparisons regarding income leveling are lacking. Should the course of the process have been less favorable in Sweden than in other countries with a similar economic and social structure (that alternative should not be excluded altogether), it would seem far-fetched to ascribe this to the employment policy pursued during the period.

In contrast to this, the traditional conflict between efforts to secure a high level of employment and the pressure to maintain economic balance is particularly acute in Sweden, for the following reasons primarily. For one thing, the political threshold of tolerance regarding unemployment, as described earlier, is lower in Sweden than in other countries with a similar social structure. For another, the institutional and organization framework of the country is such that it strengthens the Phillips relationship: wage determination goes on without government interference,[13] the rate of organization is very high, and each organization is quite centralized, while at the same time the organizational structure is split between blue-collar and white-collar groups

---

[12]*Svenska folkets inkomster* (Stockholm, 1970). An English summary of the report has been issued under the title "The Structure of Incomes in Sweden," August 1970, mimeographed.

[13] A sensational and much debated departure from the rule was made in March 1971, when the Swedish government passed a law giving it full powers to suspend conflicts that are deemed a social danger. The law was then enforced in order to interrupt a conflict in the public sector.

(with the structure of the latter in turn depending on differing principles of organization). Owing to this, the process of wage determination, which we know from experience is readily affected by fluctuations on the labor market, is given an autonomous component in the form of compensation mechanisms, which reinforce the tendencies toward wage increases.

As an extreme case, considering the level of her employment ambitions and the power of her competing labor organizations, Sweden is a suitable object for the study of the full employment–stable money value dilemma. At the same time, the country's political stability – the same party has been in power for almost four decades – and her mixed economic structure – limited government ownership, but substantial government influence on the economy – present favorable conditions in which to test, in practice, even comparatively sophisticated methods of solving conflicts of this kind.

THE INSTRUMENTS OF ECONOMIC POLICY

Given a relationship between unemployment and a rise in wages – i.e., a Phillips curve, whose position and slope are determined by a series of factors of an economic and institutional nature – the scope for a policy pursued by traditional methods is narrow for a country like Sweden. Restrictive fiscal and monetary policies elicit politically intolerable unemployment, while an expansive economic policy can lead to a rise in costs, which impairs the competitiveness and the balance on current account of the country. Attempts to solve this dilemma by means of various forms of incomes policy have had little success. In Sweden the average citizen has up to now rejected the idea of government intervention in wage determination as a matter of principle, and milder forms of incomes policy, by which responsibility for restraint as regards wages policy is left to labor organizations, have proved to be ineffective.

One attempt to solve the dilemma was made with the so-called Rehn model, the basic idea of which is to supplement an overall restrictive policy, which squeezes demand and profits, with selective measures aimed chiefly at the labor market and at regional development. Since profitability varies greatly between industries and regions, locally emerging employment problems cannot be solved by raising the overall level of demand without initiating an inflationary process. According to the model, a recession, at least a mild one, should not be counteracted by general expansive measures, which for polititical and practical reasons are put into effect too late and whose effects lag far into the phase of upswing.

Selective measures can be put into effect in time and by administrative procedure (they do not require a parliamentary decision, as does a change in taxation), they can be directed straight toward the points of the economy affected by employment problems, and they can be wound up rapidly in a phase of economic upswing.

This argument was developed as early as the late forties, when it became evident that postwar inflationary tendencies were no transient crisis feature but a permanent element in a full-employment economy.[14] The main line of thought was incorporated in a report[15] from LO (the Swedish Confederation of Trade Unions) to its 1951 congress, and thus acquired union sanction to a certain extent. This is no surprise, since the union movement, while advocating full employment, at the same time found out that inflationary tendencies hampered its efforts to achieve solidarity in wages policy. Rehn, together with Erik Lundberg, who at first was critical of the model,[16] presented his ideas to the American public in a condensed article in 1963.[17] Eventually, the model was discussed at a 1967 symposium which brought together a large number of European and American economists.[18]

Graphic illustration is the simplest way to explain Rehn's model.[19]

In Figure 5-1 the economy is composed of submarkets where the demand situation differs according to varying rates of profitability. Submarkets (which also can represent individual firms) a, b, and c are characterized by poor profitability and surplus labor; in submarkets d, e, and f, high profits, expansiveness, and labor shortage prevail. These differences are common even in a situation of overall balance, but they are more pronounced during recessions, when profits and demand for labor decline in more and more submarkets. It is then tempting for the government to raise the level of overall demand, say from BB to AA, in the hope that absorbing surplus labor will fill the gap of deficient demand. At the same time, however, excess demand is increased in already expansive submarkets, causing a higher rate of wage increase. If the Phillips curve has the shape DD (Fig. 5-2), this traditional method brings a drop in unemployment from X_0 to X_1, but a simultaneous rise in wages from Y_0 to Y_1, which may initiate a cumulative inflationary process. Rehn's alternative implies that a moderate level of demand (e.g., BB) is maintained or, in an upswing, is lowered to CC — i.e., somewhat below total equilibrium level. Employment should then be stimulated by public relief work, regional development assistance, subsidies, government orders, and other selective measures, combined with incentives for retraining and

[14] Gösta Rehn, "The Problem of Stability: An Analysis and some Public Proposals" (1948), in *Wages Policy under Full Employment*, ed. Ralph Turvey (London, 1952).

[15] *Trade Unions and Full Employment* (Malmö, 1953).

[16] Turvey, Wages Policy, pp. 55–71.

[17] G. Rehn and E. Lundberg, "Employment and Welfare: Some Swedish Issues," *Industrial Relations*, 2, no. 2 (February 1963).

[18] "Labour Market Policy and the 'Rehn Model,' " in *On Incomes Policy: Papers and Proceedings from a Conference in Honour of Erik Lundberg* (Stockholm, 1969), pp. 163–81.

[19] See R. Meidner, "Active Manpower Policy and the Inflation Unemployment Dilemma," *Swedish Journal of Economics*, September 1969.

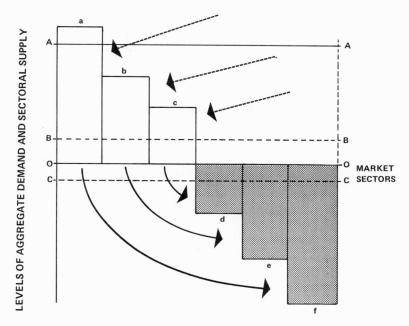

Figure 5-1. Diagram of Local Labor Markets Showing Different Supply-Demand Relations. Horizontal lines represent various levels of overall demand as determined by fiscal and monetary policy. The different levels of labor supply in different sectors are represented by the short lines *a, b, c, d, e,* and *f*. Thus, when general demand is at level O, white rectangles represent unemployment, and shaded rectangles represent excess demand for labor.

removal, which simultaneously reduce unemployment in submarkets *a, b,* and *c* and ease labor shortage in the expansive sectors *d, e,* and *f*. Dotted arrows indicate the former group of measures, continuous arrows the latter group. The purpose of this policy is to lower the Phillips curve (Fig. 5-2) to *EE* — i.e., to secure a low unemployment X_1 but at the same time to limit wage increases to Y_0.

The import of this seemingly simple model — a combination of general subduing and selective support measures — has to be analyzed more closely, however, as regards its application in a situation of uneven economic activity and structure.

To clarify the concepts "general" and "selective" in this context, we can think of full employment in the various submarkets as separate objectives of

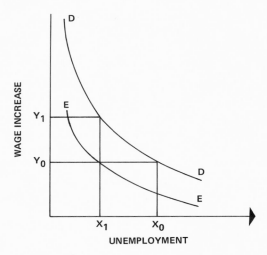

Figure 5-2. The Phillips Curve at Different Levels according
to Different Policy Mixes

economic policy. A general instrument affects the level of employment proportionally in all these submarkets, independently of the extent to which the
separate goals are attained. A selective instrument is used to influence the
level of employment directly in the submarkets where the full-employment
goal is not reached. It can either create employment within the submarket or
further mobility so that excess supply and demand even out among different
submarkets. In some cases no new decisions are needed to put the instruments to use. Mobility incentives, for instance, are often tied to an individual's employment status. When a certain employment criterion is met, the
individual automatically becomes eligible for support. It is true that in such
cases the instrument has a general character, in the sense that it is not intended for a certain group of individuals, but the effects are selective, for the
instrument is used only where employment problems crop up. "Selective"
means that a measure affects only the objective it is aimed at.

If general and selective instruments are defined this way, it is of course
impossible to find any pure examples in real life. All measures of economic
policy have direct and indirect effects on objectives other than the one aimed
at. A division into general and selective instruments cannot be absolute, but is
rather a question of differences in degree. An instrument which is intended to
be general − e.g., a change in an indirect tax − does not have exactly the
same impact on all subgoals, since elasticities, industrial structure, etc., are
different in different submarkets. The unemployment which one intends to
alleviate with a general instrument can be of quite a different nature in the

various submarkets (seasonal, cyclical, and structural unemployment). There-fore, the effects on the subgoals will vary. An instrument which is intended to operate selectively on one subgoal has direct and/or indirect effects on other goals as well. An employment-creating measure of location policy has effects outside the submarket it is aimed at.

The propensity to save, to import, etc., determines how the effects can be delimited. A thorough knowledge of the structure of the economy is neces-sary in order meaningfully to pursue a selective economic policy. Only then are there any prospects for measures that are intended to be selective actually to have selective effects. Important aids in obtaining the required knowledge may be input-output models, inquiries about household budgets, econometric models, etc. The degree of disaggregation needed in applying these aids de-pends on how many separate subgoals are subordinate to the main goals of economic policy. It is thus entirely a question of level of ambition.

In practice, it is difficult to apply the Rehn model consistently to eco-nomic policy. But this is true of any policy which is intended to pave the way for a more ambitious employment policy. The purpose, of course, is to miti-gate the conflict between high employment and economic stability, which has proved impossible to surmount with the traditional set of economic policy instruments.

With the simple Keynesian model for controlling the level of total demand, the level is soon reached at which employment objectives and price stability objectives come into conflict. The instruments of economic policy which have been available on the general level have not been fit to render goals consistent except on a relatively low level of ambition. By dividing the em-ployment goal into separate subgoals, one not only succeeds in defining the former more precisely but also provides scope for using a greater number of economic policy instruments. Although objectives of stabilization policy come into conflict on the highest level, there is still scope for action to reach the goals on a lower level. The type of selective instruments which should be used depends on the nature of the employment problem to be met. Seasonal, cyclical, and structural unemployment require different countermeasures. Seasonal unemployment is often concentrated in certain submarkets. Sub-markets with substantial structural unemployment often have an unbalanced economic structure and are therefore readily affected by cyclical variations. The course of the business cycle does not affect all submarkets in the same way. Knowledge of lags and leads may be required in order to distinguish the different types of unemployment from one another and to take the appro-priate measures to cope with them.

A well-equipped decentralized administrative machinery in overall control is a prerequisite for a successful selective policy. Owing to daily contact with regional and local problems, decentralized units are able to detect quantitative and qualitative changes in the employment situation early. On short notice labor market authorities can release a wide variety of measures, such as retraining, incentives for geographic mobility, relief work, and to a certain extent sheltered employment, location support, etc. Instruments of labor market policy proper can be synchronized with the release of investment reserve funds, government orders to industry, residential and public building, and other means, the use of which can be initiated by labor market authorities. All of these instruments cannot be handled on a completely decentralized level, for the nature of employment problems often can be estimated correctly only on the basis of the information collected from all submarkets together.

A large part of seasonal unemployment is quite easy to foresee and observe. Its demarcation in time and space is relatively well known, and action can be taken on very short notice. Here the problem is that traditional measures, particularly relief work, are difficult to interrupt when employment is again offered in the previous occupation. In the long run, the quantitative importance of seasonal unemployment is decreasing as new methods of production are introduced and year-round employment becomes the rule (e.g., in the forestry and building industries).

The biggest problem may well be to distinguish secular and structural disturbances from transient, cyclical ones. Provided that the correct diagnosis of the nature of the disturbance can be made, several selective employment policy measures have the advantage (as compared to general measures) of greater precision, in terms of the target aimed at, and better possibilities to shorten time lags. The observation lag can be shortened. The administrative decision lag becomes shorter, since no protracted parliamentary discussion is needed except in decisions of principle regarding new instruments of economic policy to be put at the disposal of labor market authorities. Decisions can also be quicker because the information collected is more relevant to the solution of the problem. The operation lag – the time that passes before the measure taken actually affects the level of employment – is presumably shorter if the measure is directed straight at the deviation from the employment target of a particular labor submarket than if it is aimed at the commodity market or the credit market or at all labor submarkets together. In the latter case, other means must be put into effect to counter departures from employment targets caused by the initial measure, and these means again have repercussions on the variable initially disturbed. Even if the measure is directed straight at the disturbance, undesirable effects on the other target variables ensue, but these are of a more limited range than they would be if the measure were given a general form.

The risk of improper timing of economic policy decreases if selective means are given more scope in economic policy. This risk diminishes not only because the lag is shorter but also because the many relatively small measures produce a spread of risks, since they can be adapted to the disparate cyclical phases on the various labor submarkets. Keeping in mind the serious consequences of improper timing of policy for the prospects of pursuing stabilization policy in an economy which constantly swings from weak recessions to quite vigorous expansion, this diminished risk is very important.

But the distinction between selective and general policies should not be exaggerated. They should be considered complementary rather than mutually exclusive alternatives. In a situation where economic policy must counteract recession and stimulate expansion generally, it is desirable to use means which have larger multiplier effects. However, these traditional instruments of expansive fiscal and monetary policy need the firm support of selective employment-creating measures. In a situation of restraint of the overall level of demand, there is no scope for general expansive means, and the emphasis of selective policy will shift from employment-creating means to adjustment-promoting means. In a situation characterized by a low level of general unemployment, unemployment is largely structural and frictional. In this context structural means that manpower demanded and manpower available do not correspond. This lack of correspondence can have various dimensions — e.g., geographic and occupational. In this situation mobility-promoting instruments can further adjustment. Mobility policy must aim at both capital and manpower, but in Sweden it has until now largely been limited to manpower. Limited location-policy action, scattered over a great number of places, cannot create any alternative to manpower mobility. In order to avoid direct conflict with the goal regarding economic growth, action must focus on so called growth centers, where positive external effects and economies of scale related to social capital can be taken advantage of. In such growth centers, retraining should not necessarily be the first step taken toward geographic removal and individual welfare losses, although it often has been in the past. On the basis of our knowledge of regional employment multipliers, it is also possible to give employment policy such a form as to avoid reinforcing the process toward uneconomic geographic concentration. Instead, employment policy can be aimed at relieving the pressure of bottlenecks in production.

Both selective and general measures are to a great extent financed through the budget. The combined action of a great number of selective measures elicit expansive multiplying effects, which, in a given cyclical phase, must be offset by general measures. The proportion of selective and general means can be varied according to circumstances. The mix will depend on the degree of utilization of capacity which prevails in the economy at the time of decision. The relationship is illustrated in Figure 5-3, where the different positions U_1, U_2, and U_3 stand for successively greater levels of unemployment in different phases of the business cycle, and the isoquant lines indicate alternative policy mixes relative to the given level of unemployment. Along curve *B*, which denotes a more selective policy than does curve *A*, a gradual transition occurs from employment-creating to adjustment-promoting measures when we move from U_3 to U_2 and U_1. Because the quantitative variation in general methods is smaller in alternative *B*, the risk of improper timing diminishes there and the impact on the employment goal increases. But freedom of choice among various alternatives is restricted by our knowledge of the effects of the instruments.

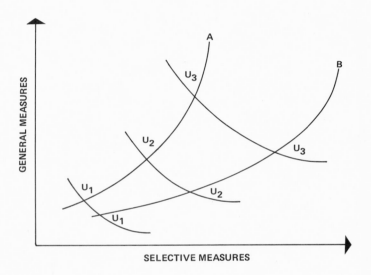

Figure 5-3. Mix of General and Selective Measures at Various
Levels of Unemployment

Thus it is evident that the boundary lines between general and selective measures waver, particularly as soon as the latter are applied on a large scale. Still, the Rehn model retains its conceptual distinctiveness and offers a realistic alternative to traditional anticyclical stabilization policy with fiscal and monetary policy as main instruments. The innovation, from the point of view of stabilization policy, is the role attributed to labor market policy in the Rehn model, not the means of labor market policy, which at least nowadays are widely used in many countries. When we speak of "the new labor market policy" which has existed in Sweden since the late fifties, we do not mean that new instruments have been created, but rather that already known instruments have gradually been used more and more extensively and explicitly for stabilization and structural policy purposes. Therefore, the description of the Swedish labor market policy arsenal can be kept very brief.[20]

The expansion of labor market policy can easily be visualized from the growing share of the state budget and of the Gross National Product taken by labor market policy expenditures, as noted in Table 5-1.

Table 5-1. Labor Market Administration Expenditures in Sweden, 1950–1970

Year	As % of Budget	As % of Swedish GNP
1950	1.0	0.2
1955	1.1	0.2
1960	3.7	0.9
1965	3.5	1.0
1970	5.6	1.4

Of greater interest than these figures, which, in spite of their doubling many times over during a twenty-year period, give an impression of very limited range, is the shift of emphasis from employment policy measures in a more traditional sense (both socially motivated and employment-creating measures) and action designed to facilitate the adjustment of manpower. The turning point apparently came in the early sixties. The share of employment-creating measures which emphasize public relief work decreased substantially after 1960, the proportion of socially motivated expenditures increased, and measures which make up the core of the new labor market policy — training and mobility incentives — show a vigorous upward trend. Still, at the end of the period, they accounted for no more than a surprisingly small part of total Labor Market Administration expenditures and for a far smaller part than did relief work. See Table 5-2.

We get a different and, from a labor market policy standpoint, more accurate picture when studying developments as to the number of persons involved in various activities. All series show a sharp increase from the early

[20]The instruments of Swedish labor market policy have previously been presented extensively in a series of publications, some of which are: OECD, *Labour Market Policy in Sweden* (Paris, 1963); *Modern Swedish Labour Market Policy: A Government Policy in Sweden* (Stockholm, 1966); B. Olsson, "Employment Policy in Sweden," *International Labour Review*, 87 (1963): 5; *idem*, "Labour Market Policy in Modern Society," in *Toward a Manpower Policy*, ed. R. A. Gordon (New York, 1967); and Ragnar Sohlman, "The Rapid Action Aspect of Swedish Labour Market Policy," paper presented at the Conference on Employment Fluctuations and Manpower Policy, OECD, Paris, 1969, mimeographed.

Table 5-2. The Distribution of Labor Market Policy according to
Various Categories of Measures, 1950-1970

(as % of total expenditure)

Year	Employment-Creating Measures[a]	Socially Motivated Measures[b]	Training and Incentives to Mobility	Employment Service & Administration
1950	19.1	38.4	1.3	41.2
1955	30.1	43.0	0.3	26.6
1960	70.6	16.2	5.0	8.2
1965	52.7	24.7	12.1	10.5
1968/69	34.8	39.2	17.3	8.7
1969/70	32.4	38.9	17.6	11.1

[a] Public relief work, regional development loans, and grants.
[b] Vocational rehabilitation, archival work, assistance to refugees, and cash assistance.

fifties on, but the rise is explosive as regards labor market retraining. At the
end of the period almost 1 percent of the labor force on the average was in
training, nearly 2 percent (about the same as the registered unemployed) was
employed through the Labor Market Administration, and a good 4 percent of
the labor force was affected by some kind of labor market policy measure,
with emphasis on retraining and mobility incentives. As expressed in the
number of persons involved, the "new labor market policy" can now be said
to be of more than marginal importance. Add to this the employment service,
which in Sweden is estimated to provide 25 percent of placements, though
apparently a lesser share during the above period. See Table 5-3.

A survey of the Swedish labor market policy arsenal would be incomplete
were no mention made of investment reserve funds — i.e., funds to which
tax-free allocations of profits are allowed in phases of boom. Funds are
released by decision of the government for investment during recessions or in
industrially less developed areas, at which time taxes are levied but at a lower
rate. The system, which because of the tax reduction, is of particular interest
to expansive and profitable firms, has played a substantial part in leveling
investment activities, and thereby employment as well, throughout the business cycle.[21]

THE MODEL IN PRACTICE

Cyclical fluctuations during the postwar period have been mild in Sweden
compared to both the interwar period and to fluctuations in other countries

[21] See G. Eliasson, *Investment Funds in Operation* (Stockholm, 1965).

Table 5-3. Number of Persons Subjected to
Labor Market Measures, 1950-1970

Year	Public Relief Work	Vocational Rehabilitation, Archival Work, Sheltered Workshops	Labor Market Training		Total Employed by LMA (1 + 2 + 3)	
			Annual Average	Total	Total	As % of Labor Force
	1	2	3	4	5	6
1950	1,053	1,413	250	570	2,716	0.1
1955	996	2,411	500	979	3,907	0.1
1960	5,778	5,182	6,580	11,800	17,540	0.5
1965	9,824	9,875	15,922	46,002	35,621	0.9
1970	15,580	ca. 20,800	33,883	107,695[a]	ca. 69,300	1.8

Year	Number of Persons Who Received Starting Allowance	Total Number of Persons Affected by LMA Measures (1 + 2 + 4 + 7)		Number of Placements by Employment Service (thousands)	Registered Insured Unemployed as % of Total Insured	% Unemployed According to Labor Force Survey
		Total Number	As % of Labor Force			
	7	8	9	10	11	12
1950	—	3,036	0.1	1,196	—	—
1955	—	4,386	0.1	1,030	1.5[b]	—
1960	6,950	29,710	0.8	942	1.4	1.5
1965	21,144	86,845	2.3	920	1.1	1.2
1970	23,547	166,600	4.3	—	1.5	1.5

[a] Refers to budget year 1970/71.
[b] Refers to 1956.

in Western Europe.[22] The rather mild recessions of 1958-59, 1962, and 1967-68 reflect periods of contracting activity in Western Europe and can, as far as Sweden is concerned, be attributed to a falling rate of exports (actually, except for 1958, to a slower rate of increase). Fluctuations in the volume of exports have evidently affected the whole economy — primarily gross investment, employment, and, although to a limited degree, Gross National Product. The most remarkable features are the invariably low level of registered unemployment all through the sixties, with only an insignificant rise during the recession years 1967-68, and the quite stable rate of participation; but in both instances stability conceals shifting trends for subgroups. A historical record of these economic data, however, does not show to what extent em-

[22] See the extensive analysis by Erik Lundberg, *Instability and Economic Growth* (New Haven and London, 1968).

ployment stabilization resulted from deliberate anticyclical and employment-supporting measures, even though significant variations in exports (from 0 percent to 13 percent) and in private investment activities (from −1½ percent to +10 percent) give a hint of it. See Table 5-4.

Table 5-4. Main Components of the Swedish Economy, 1956-1970

(percentages)

Year	GNP in Constant Prices[a]	Volume of Exports[a]	Private Gross Invest-ment[a]	Registered Insured Unem-ployed as % of Total Insured	Unem-ployed as % of Labor Force	Labor Force Partici-pation Rate	Consumer Prices[a]
1956	3.5	10.2	3.4	1.5	–	–	4.5
1957	2.9	8.2	0.3	1.9	–	–	4.3
1958	1.4	−0.6	7.0	2.5	–	–	4.8
1959	5.7	7.7	7.1	2.0	–	–	0.7
1960	3.7	13.1	9.9	1.4	–	–	3.9
1961	5.1	5.8	9.7	1.2	–	60.5	2.5
1962	3.8	8.2	1.2	1.3	–	61.3	4.3
1963	4.9	8.3	3.5	1.4	1.5	61.4	2.9
1964	6.9	11.4	3.2	1.1	1.4	60.9	3.4
1965	3.8	4.8	5.0	1.1	1.2	61.2	5.0
1966	3.0	6.2	9.6	1.4	1.6	60.6	6.3
1967	3.3	6.4	−1.4	1.7	2.0	59.8	4.5
1968	3.5	8.2	−4.0	2.0	2.0	60.6	1.9
1969	4.0	12.0	4.0	1.7	1.6	60.6	2.8
1970	4.5	8.5	10.0	1.4	1.5	–	6.8

[a]Change in percentage since the previous year.

In the following section we shall discuss the interplay of general and selective stabilization measures. But first — the prospect of empirically testing the question of whether the Rehn model has been put to use is actually limited — the reader should be reminded of a basic idea behind the model: that there must be, from the viewpoint of stabilization, an optimal mix of general and selective measures. One extreme is traditional Keynesian policy, which is intended to influence a homogeneous market economy by expanding and contracting purchasing power; this extreme virtually limits our choice to either too much inflation or too much unemployment. The other extreme is a policy which, based on the knowledge that a receding economy is disparate and that the functioning of the market is imperfect, mainly relies on selective measures. The latter alternative would ultimately lead to a thoroughly regulated economy and is therefore rejected for political reasons. *But, between those extremes, where is the optimal (from a stabilization and employment point of view), and at the same time politically acceptable, combination?*

Let us, with reference to Figure 5-3, illustrate the desirable level of employment (e.g., a certain rate of participation, or, for practical purposes, a rate of unemployment, which can be tolerated) with an isoquant line on which each position corresponds to a conceivable combination of total demand (excess or deficient) and selective manpower policy (Fig. 5-4). The convex shape of the isoquant line expresses the hypothesis that there are diminishing returns in the use of both general measures and labor market policies (see Appendix, especially pp. 154–55, 157). At point *a* of the figure a strong excess demand prevails: expected profits are high, part of the "hard core of unemployment" is absorbed by production, tendencies toward wage drift are strong. The task of labor market policy is confined to creating employment opportunities for labor whose productivity is low (the poorly skilled, older, or handicapped in some way) and in areas where few employment opportunities exist. Such a combination can be imagined to correspond to the Phillips curve *DD* in Figure 5-2 — i.e., level of employment X_1 leads to wage increase Y_1, which initiates a cumulative inflationary process. A reduction of total demand below the equilibrium to point *b* in Figure 5-4 is possible only (retaining the same high level of employment) when the volume of selective measures is expanded to l_2. Here expectations of profits and wage drift are restrained; the combination $d_2 l_2$ can be seen to correspond to a lower Phillips curve, say *EE* in Figure 5-2, where the desired level of employment X_1 (selective measures are assumed to secure employment for a significantly greater number of persons threatened by unemployment than would the combination $d_1 l_1$) is accompanied by a more limited rise in prices Y_0, which is considered to be consistent with economic balance.

This type of model, with its very high demands upon flexibility, well-timed and purposeful action, and highly developed labor market policy, is difficult to convert into a concrete stabilization program. Certain authoritative statements suggest, however, that since the late fifties the Swedish government has been aiming at the model and has, in some cyclical downswings, preferred a mix of general and selective measures to traditional expansive policy with general means only.

Thus the minister of finance declared in 1958 that slackening demand derived from falling exports should not be offset by the general expansion of domestic demand. To cope with unemployment, vigorous action must be taken to transfer dismissed workers to still-expansive areas without resorting to generally demand-raising policy — *"in other words selective labor market policy is brought to the fore."*[23] A year later, when recession still prevailed,

---

[23] Sweden, Finance Bill, 1958, budget statement, p. 15; italics added.

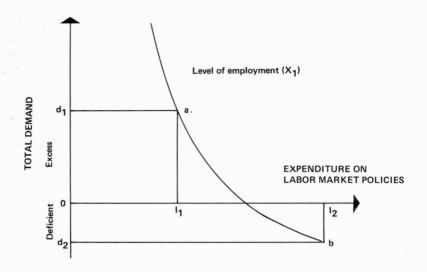

Figure 5-4. Relationship between Total Demand and
Selective Manpower Policy

the minister of finance held the opinion that an increasing deficit in the
budget reflected the adjustment of fiscal policy to the level of economic
activity — in accordance with the principles of fiscal policy which had prevailed since the early thirties — but again selective measures were stressed:
increased residential building, release of investment reserve funds, tariff increases for textiles, and enlargement of government-owned industrial enterprises.[24] In a commentary on the budget for 1959 the minister of finance
formulated his policy in terms which fully correspond to the basic idea in the
Rehn model: What is required is not a general restraint of demand but stimuli
to exposed sectors in the shape of selective measures.[25]

The next two years — 1960 and 1961 — were years of booming activity,
and government borrowing was restrained for stabilization purposes. A definite innovation was the statement of 1960 that labor market policy should be
just as active in upswings and focus on adjustment measures to make for
smoother structural change.[26] Removal of labor, which during recessions is
enforced by unemployment, requires substantial public incentives in times of
boom.[27]

[24]*Ibid.*, 1959.
[25]*Nationalekonomiska Föreningens förhandlingar* [Proceedings of the Swedish
Economic Association], 1959, no. 1.
[26]*Ibid.*, 1960, no. 1.
[27]*Ibid.*, 1961, no. 1.

In 1962, economic activity showed signs of abating, and unemployment was slightly higher. In his account of developments during that year, the minister of finance asserted with satisfaction that the restraint imposed by fiscal policy had not eased and that the budget had remained fairly neutral. The disparity in the level of activity among various sectors of the economy had illustrated the importance of an active labor market policy.[28]

In the following years the theme (with variations) of the significant task of labor market policy in periods of boom continued to be to even out disparities among submarkets, mainly through removal grants, retraining, relief work, and the selective use of investment reserve funds.[29] But in his commentary on the budget statement of 1965 the minister of finance admitted the failure to repress inflationary tendencies: the budget had grown less restrictive as a consequence of "political realities." A certain resignation as regards the applicability of the Rehn model could be detected in the statement that, between the alternatives of inflation at a rate of 3 percent a year and unemployment, it was not definite that the anti-inflationary line of policy would be preferred in the long run.[30]

The recession period of 1967–68 elicited new statements to the effect that the government intended to meet the slack in the economy not with general demand stimulating measures but with increased support to mobility.[31] In the budget statement of 1968 the minister of finance emphasized more strongly than ever before that, in spite of increasing unemployment, domestic demand must be controlled, and, at the same time, greatly increased resources must be put at the disposal of labor market and regional development policy. Fiscal policies should be resorted to only if international demand turns out to be lower than expected. Labor market policy was explicitly declared an *effective part of an active anticyclical and stabilization policy.*[32]

Since 1968 the importance of continued expansion of labor market policy under booms has repeatedly been proclaimed; primarily its task is to even out regional differences and to provide support for older and handicapped persons. The minister of finance, however, has been forced to admit that the cyclical upswing of 1969 came about unexpectedly and that fiscal policy apparently had not been restrictive enough.[33] But faced with a new contraction in 1971, we find once more a firm declaration of principle: a general relaxation of economic policy is inappropriate; slackening demand should be countered by selective measures.[34]

[28] Sweden, Finance Bill, 1963.
[29] *Ibid.*, 1964.
[30] *Nationalekonomiska Föreningens förhandlingar*, 1965, no. 1.
[31] *Ibid.*, 1967, no. 1.
[32] Sweden, Finance Bill, 1968.
[33] *Nationalekonomiska Föreningens förhandlingar*, 1970, no. 1.
[34] Sweden, Finance Bill, 1971.

The pattern in the Swedish government's statements is quite clear: at the prospect of recession, adherence to the principle that unemployment problems must not be solved by general measures to augment purchasing power is professed emphatically. During periods of cyclical upswing and of boom, when budget policy has recurrently proved to be too weak to curb overheating and inflationary tendencies, expansion of labor market policy is recommended as a means to even out regional and sectoral imbalance. In other words, the Swedish government recommends a constant enlargement of labor market policy programs that stress employment-creating measures during recessions and adjustment-promoting measures during booms. The question, however, is how this model has been transformed into practical policy.

In a previous section we discussed the question of whether a redistribution of stabilization policy measures in favor of a larger proportion of selective instruments could have positive stabilizing effects. It is impossible to answer this question on the basis of the empirical material available. We can observe that the resources allocated to labor market policy have increased strongly during the fifties and the sixties. Their share of the expenditures of the state budget has increased more than five fold. This share has not been growing smoothly, however; on the contrary, the rate of increase has varied very much, and oscillations have coincided with upswings and downswings of the economic cycle. In 1961 the budget of the Labor Market Administration was cut by 43 percent when a feeble tendency of overheating prevailed. (See Table 5-5.)

Table 5-5. Expenditures of the Labor Market Administration as a Percentage of the (State) Budget

Year	%	Year	%
1948	0.84	1959	3.68
1949	1.15	1960	3.73
1950	0.96	1961	2.30
1951	0.87	1962	2.25
1952	0.72	1963	3.39
1953	0.95	1964	3.53
1954	1.21	1965	3.47
1955	1.11	1966/67	3.85
1956	1.25	1967/68	4.65
1957	1.62	1968/69	5.38
1958	2.22	1969/70	5.48

Too few observations are available to prove statistically a changed relationship between labor market policy resources and the use of general instruments. As mentioned previously, all labor market policy instruments cannot simply be declared selective; nor can other instruments of economic policy be presumed not to have selective effects. Moreover, we cannot establish whether results of economic policy can be explained by changed proportions of selective and general measures. There is no method by which to calculate the magnitude of the disturbances incurred by the economy with a given impact of economic policy.

A study by Lars Matthiessen indicates that the impact of fiscal policy on total real demand, as a percentage of GNP, shows smaller and smaller variations (Fig. 5-5). The net impact is calculated as the sum of the effects of fiscal measures, changes in public demand, and automatic fiscal changes. Calculations are not based on an econometric model, for no reliable, sufficiently disaggregated model exists for Sweden. Therefore, indirect effects on investment have been indicated only qualitatively in the figure, with arrows giving the direction in which they work.

The net impact of fiscal policy has converged toward zero. The weak and belated contracting action put in against the overheating of 1964-65, the failure of expanding measures put in against the lengthy recession of 1966-68, and the statements of the government about the priority accorded to selective policy indicate that traditional Keynesian fiscal policy has become less significant in Sweden.

DEGREE OF EFFECTIVENESS

As suggested in the previous sections, Sweden's employment goal — never a clearly fixed target, but rather a rolling, more and more ambitious objective — has been realized to a greater extent than has her stabilization goal. In the ensuing section we shall qualify this opinion and analyze the causes of the uneven results.

Has Full Employment Been Maintained during the Period?

Unemployment, as measured the conventional way (insured unemployed registered with employment services as a percentage of total insured) has been low during the period (see Table 5-4, p. 134), with small variations occurring only between booms and recessions. The latter are clearly discernible in 1957-59 (to be precise, from the spring of 1957 to the spring of 1959) and in 1967-68. As measured by the labor force survey method, unemployment is constantly slightly higher, but it follows the same pattern.

It is more interesting, however, to examine whether cyclical fluctuations have had an impact on labor force participation rates. In a number of Western European countries the reduction of the number of persons in the labor force has been more important during the gravest recessions of the late sixties than the rise in the rate of registered unemployment.[35] To test the hypothesis that

[35] "Sometimes this hidden increase of unemployment seems to be even bigger than that registered" (OECD), *Implementation of the OECD Council Recommendation on Active Manpower Policy* (Paris, 1968), p. 4.

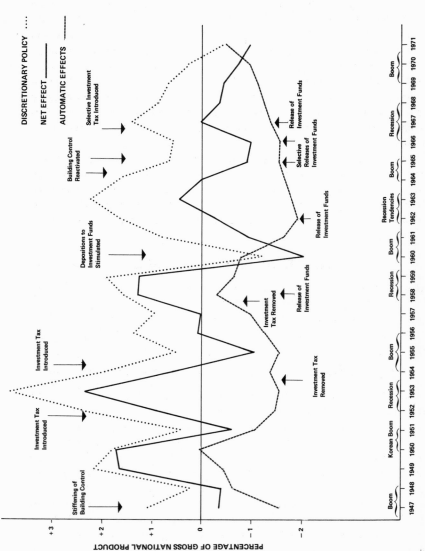

Figure 5-5. Impact of Fiscal Policy on Aggregate Demand as a Percentage of GNP (From Erik Lundberg *et al., Svensk finanspolitik i teori och praktik* [Swedish Fiscal Policy

this may have been true also in Sweden, the total in the sixth column of Table 5-4 must be disaggregated. Actually, the apparent stability conceals significant fluctuations among subgroups.

The hypothesis is that youths, women (married women in particular), and older persons may be forced to leave the labor force in a slackening phase of the business cycle. The lower age groups should be kept out of the analysis, however, since powerful educational expansion was characteristic of the sixties and has resulted in a substantial reduction in the number of persons in the labor force. How the unemployment and participation rates developed during the years 1961-70 for various categories according to sex, marital status, and age is shown in Table 5-6. It should be noted that in some cases relative unemployment rates are based on such small numbers that figures are uncertain.

There is a marked increase in the level of unemployment of most subgroups during the recession of 1967-68, particularly as regards the higher age groups. No remarkable rise in the level of unemployment of married women can be detected. It is difficult to interpret fluctuations in the participation rate. If we focus our attention on the years 1967-68, we notice that the rate of participation is very high and variations are small for men between twenty-five and fifty-four years of age. The decline during recession is — surprisingly enough — most obvious for younger men, for whom a falling trend can be seen during the late sixties, possibly due to a prolongation of education and training. A distinct cyclical pattern can be seen concerning the thirty-five to forty-four age group, which has the highest average participation rate; the decline in the years 1967-68 is pronounced (a good 2 percent) and is followed by a clear recovery by the end of the decade. Thus, during the recession, disguised unemployment appears to have increased more than declared unemployment for this group. The same tendency, though to a lesser degree, can be seen in the fifty-five to sixty-four age group. There, recession caused no reduction in the rate of participation of men, but a strong decline occurred during the boom of 1969-70. This, it can be assumed, resulted from an accelerating structural change in the Swedish economy and from the growing employment problems of older workers which derived from it. This impression is reinforced by a look at the highest age group: their participation rate has fallen since 1962, and in marked steps in 1963 and 1966 — that is to say, years of incipient employment problems. The fact that the decline continued during 1969 may support the hypothesis that older workers encounter increasing difficulties in an economy characterized by rapid structural transformation. Gradually improved pension benefits may, of course, have aided older persons to leave the labor force more or less voluntarily to a larger extent than previously.

As regards unmarried women, there is a great disparity among subgroups: for younger women and women below the age of forty-five, whose rate of

Table 5-6. Rates of Unemployment (A) and Participation (B) in Various
Categories according to Age, Sex, and Marital Status,
1961–1970

Age Group		1961	1962	1963	1964	1965	1966	1967	1968	1969	1970
25–34											
Men	A	1.9	0.9	1.0	1.0	0.6	0.7	1.6	1.8	1.0	0.9
	B	94.0	95.7	94.8	96.1	95.4	95.4	94.5	94.4	93.1	93.5
Single Women	A	2.8	2.8	1.7	0.9	0	3.2	3.7	1.7	1.4	1.8
	B	80.7	82.4	84.0	78.7	80.8	80.4	81.7	83.3	80.9	82.2
Married Women	A	1.5	1.3	3.3	2.5	2.4	2.3	1.3	2.4	2.1	2.4
	B	40.4	47.4	50.0	44.9	48.4	45.5	45.6	50.7	53.5	56.9
35–44											
Men	A	1.2	0.4	0.2	0.6	0.7	0.7	1.3	1.0	0.7	0.8
	B	99.3	97.3	97.2	96.1	97.5	97.8	95.8	95.5	96.4	96.3
Single Women	A	0	3.2	0.8	0.8	3.0	1.9	1.5	3.8	1.8	0.7
	B	82.9	82.5	83.4	77.4	74.1	77.2	79.1	82.3	81.0	82.5
Married Women	A	1.9	1.4	1.9	2.8	3.0	1.6	0	2.0	1.6	0.9
	B	47.9	49.7	51.2	55.0	55.4	58.3	59.3	59.7	63.2	66.8
45–54											
Men	A	0.4	1.2	1.0	0.8	0.3	1.6	0.9	0.9	0.7	0.8
	B	96.7	96.6	96.9	96.0	96.6	95.4	95.8	94.4	94.7	94.6
Single Women	A	1.1	1.3	1.3	1.1	1.9	0.6	1.3	0.7	1.3	0.7
	B	82.0	72.3	75.2	77.6	75.0	77.4	75.9	74.3	77.9	78.8
Married Women	A	3.5	0.5	2.6	0.9	1.2	0.9	1.9	1.3	1.7	1.2
	B	47.8	52.3	53.0	52.3	52.4	56.2	55.9	57.4	60.4	64.5
55–64											
Men	A	1.5	3.0	1.4	0.7	1.1	1.8	1.5	2.8	1.3	1.6
	B	86.3	88.2	90.0	88.4	88.4	88.7	89.6	89.3	86.6	85.0
Single Women	A	1.2	1.1	1.1	0	1.1	0.5	0.8	0.6	1.3	1.8
	B	55.0	48.6	59.4	55.0	53.0	56.1	51.6	51.0	53.1	55.2
Married Women	A	1.0	0	1.4	0.5	0	0.8	0.5	0.8	1.3	1.7
	B	31.7	30.3	35.0	30.6	33.9	38.8	38.3	38.2	40.6	40.5
65+											
Men	A	1.2	2.1	1.2	4.1	1.3	0.8	2.9	4.5	2.2	–
	B	28.7	32.8	30.3	30.7	27.5	24.9	24.4	24.9	22.6	–
Single Women	A	0	0	0	0	0	0	0	4.0	0.9	–
	B	6.1	11.2	7.7	6.9	9.7	5.3	4.8	6.2	6.2	–
Married Women	A	0	0	0	0	0	0	3.1	3.0	2.4	–
	B	4.7	7.5	6.5	8.0	6.0	6.1	4.8	7.2	5.9	–

Source: Sweden, National Central Bureau of Statistics.

participation normally is high (over 80 percent), the recession of 1967–68 was not detrimental. The opposite was true of older women. For the age group forty-five to fifty-four, of which up to 80 percent are gainfully employed, labor participation fell by 2 to 3 percentage points, then rose to the normal level of the group during the ensuing boom. It should be noted that the rise in the level of open unemployment was slight for this group during the years of recession. The slack was disastrous for the least attractive groups on the labor market, older unmarried women. For the fifty-five to sixty-four age group, whose normal rate of participation is a good 50 percent, a decrease of about 5 percentage points occurred in 1967-68 — i.e., about 10 percent of the whole group was pushed out of the labor market during the recession. As a percentage, the decline was still greater for the oldest group of unmarried women, a group which is only loosely connected to the labor market. In 1967 the rate of participation for this group was only half that of 1965, a year of boom, and recovery in 1968-69 was feeble.

The evolution of the rate of participation of married women in the labor force is dominated by a strong upward trend for all age groups except the highest one. The slackening of economic activity in 1966-68 is reflected by a decrease for the youngest women and by a distinct retardation for the other age groups. The trend is remarkably uniform for women between the ages of thirty-five and sixty-four — i.e., for groups past the phase of child care — while the rate of increase is slightly slower for young women. Cyclical retardation is evident in this long-run development, which is related to urbanization, growth of the service sector, deliberate attempts to facilitate gainful employment of married women through collective child supervision, and a different view of the work of women.

The result of this examination can now be summed up. The rise in the level of visible unemployment does not fully reflect the changes in employment which occurred in connection with the recession of the late sixties. The stability of the aggregate rate of participation, which varied very little during the only period of real recession of the sixties, actually conceals the fact that, while certain groups are readily affected by fluctuations of the business cycle, variations for these groups have been offset by an upward trend for other groups. The fall in the rate of participation in 1967-68, which resulted from a cyclical downswing, was substantial for men in the thirty-five to forty-four age group, for men over sixty-five, and for unmarried women over forty-five. For married women, recessions have slowed down the strong increase in the rate of participation which went on all through the sixties (from less than 40 percent to more than 50 percent). With some exceptions, the rise of visible unemployment for these groups was negligible. We must conclude, then, that, in spite of an ambitious employment objective and an extensive labor market policy, Sweden has not been able to prevent falling demand — deriving primarily from slackening exports and private investment activity — from severely affecting certain groups. The rise in the level of unemployment has been moderate, but a far greater number than the registered unemployed have been forced to leave the labor force. However, this phenomenon has been much more limited in scope in Sweden than in a number of Western European countries. Furthermore, no exceptionally high emigration of foreign manpower occurred, although immigration declined substantially in 1967.

The fact that registered unemployment has been kept low during the postwar period and that the participation rate could be stabilized for most groups in years of recession and was forced down only slightly for the others (with just a few exceptions) gives no plain answer to the question of whether Sweden, even in cyclical upswings, has reached full employment in the sense of the ILO convention: full, productive, and freely chosen employment for all who want employment. A number of special studies indicate that, even in Sweden, where the level of ambition in employment policy is high, substantial underemployment exists.

By means of a number of questions added to the regular labor force survey, the governmental Commission of Inquiry into Low Income Groups has collected data about the number of jobseekers in 1966.[36] The results are shown in Table 5-7. Thus, open unemployment (equals jobseekers) was significant among the lower age groups, and, according to the commission, the lower figures for higher age groups should be interpreted with caution, since many people leave the labor force after a period of useless search for work. Nearly 10 percent of the Swedish people were unemployed for some period of time during 1966. The median duration of unemployment — the same for men and women — was about 7½ weeks, which corresponds to a rate of unemployment at any particular time of the year of less than 1½ percent — i.e., a figure which may lead to the premature conclusion that unemployment has practically ceased to be a problem in Sweden.

Table 5-7. Persons Who Were Unemployed for at Least One Week during 1966, by Age and Sex

(as % of the labor force)

Age	Men	Women	Average
14–19 years	12	11	11
20–24	11	11	11
25–34	10	11	10
35–44	6	9	7
45–54	8	8	8
55–66	8	5	7
67–74	5	4	5
Average	8	9	9

The Commission on Low Incomes also attempted to estimate the extent of disguised unemployment. Its estimate included women who were not gainfully employed or who worked only part of the year because they found it difficult to arrange for child care, part-time workers looking for full-time

---

[36]*Svenska folkets inkomster* [The Structure of Incomes in Sweden], report submitted by the Commission of Inquiry into Low Income Groups, SOU 1970:34 (Stockholm, 1970).

jobs, and the so-called latently unemployed (persons who do not actively seek work but who state their willingness to accept an offer of employment). The result was a rate of disguised unemployment of at least the same size as the figure for open unemployment quoted above.

It is obvious that the inclusion of disguised unemployment stretches the concept of unemployment to the point that it becomes "unutilized labor potential" rather than unemployment in the conventional sense. The commission's estimates of underemployment, however, are confirmed by current labor force surveys, which, apart from open unemployment, also account for "latent jobseekers" and the "underemployed" (see Table 5-8).

Table 5-8. Labor Potential in Sweden according to the
Labor Force Survey in the Fall of 1969

(as % of the several groups over fourteen years of age)

	Men	Women Married	Women Unmarried	Average
1. Not in the labor force	25.7	50.6	56.4	39.4
2. Of these: not in the labor force because of studies, household work, military service, or incapacity for work	14.8	46.7	45.0	30.6
3. "Others" not in the labor force	10.9	3.9	11.4	8.8
4. "Latently unemployed"[a]	0.8	5.6	2.3	2.5
5. Unemployed	0.9	0.9	1.3	1.0
6. "Underemployed"[b]	1.2	2.7	1.3	1.5
7. Total (4 + 5 + 6)	2.9	9.2	4.9	5.0
8. Unemployed registered with employment services[c]	—	—	—	1.2
9. Persons involved in manpower programs[d]	—	—	—	2.3

Source: Sweden, Central Bureau of Statistics and Labor Market Administration.

[a]Persons who would have sought employment had they thought they could find a suitable job where they lived.
[b]Persons who worked less than thirty-five hours a week, but who were willing and able to work more during the relevant period.
[c]Average for September–November.
[d]Persons in training programs, relief work, sheltered workshops, and "archival work."

Even with the narrower definition of "latent" or "potential" unemployment which is used in labor force surveys, and taking into account that in the fall of 1969 the employment situation was slightly better than that in 1966, the observation stands that latent unemployment and underemployment are many times greater than open unemployment. To this should be added the fact that, on the average, 2 percent of the labor force is involved in manpower programs (see Table 5-3).

The Labor Market Board carried out an investigation of the population not in the labor force[37] in 1969. The inquiry revealed that a good one-fourth of the population of aged fourteen to seventy-four was outside the labor force during the whole year (39 percent of the women and 14 percent of the men). Nine-tenths of all persons who gave studies as a reason for being outside the labor force were under 25 years of age; only about 5,000 participated in adult education. Thus the considerable expansion of adult education in Sweden has not led to any decline in the participation rate for adults. In fact, undereducation might be at the root of lower participation. As regards ill health as an obstacle to work, a strong relationship with educational level can be observed: the share of persons who cannot work because of ill health is four times greater among those with an elementary education only than among those with a higher education. The same tendency is found for the numerous women who are outside the labor force because of household duties. It is tempting to conclude that the reasons designated as "illness" and "household work" partly hide labor market characteristics — in other words, that a relatively high proportion of persons with a low level of education are really underemployed. In a similar way the study established the existence of regional underemployment: 16 percent of the men and no less than 45 percent of the women in the so-called forest counties were outside the labor force, as compared with 13 percent and 34 percent respectively, in urban counties. Even if these differences to a certain extent reflect dissimilarity in age and educational structure, they are mainly a sign of real underemployment in regions with a poorly developed economy and a deficient demand for labor. See Table 5-9.

Table 5-9. Main Causes for Being Outside the Labor Force
during the Whole of 1969

(as % of the total group)

Cause	Men	Women	Married Women
Studies	31	11	1
Ill Health	29	14	10
Household Work	0	54	75
Retired (pensioned)	36	17	9
Lack of Work	0	2	3
Others	4	2	2
Total	100	100	100

The material accounted for in this section must be treated with caution when it comes to interpreting figures for registered unemployment. Latent unemployment is about equal to open unemployment. But underemploy-

[37]Clas Almén, "Personer utanför arbetskraften 1969" [Persons Not in the Labor Force, 1969], 1971, mimeographed.

ment — which is not even designated as "latent unemployment," and which can be read off the educationally and regionally diversified participation rates — should in turn be even higher and should vary with cyclical fluctuations. By international standards, employment is high in Sweden, open unemployment is unusually low, and labor market policy programs are substantial. But not even a society with such ambitious objectives as Sweden has, has managed to eliminate underemployment derived from structural, regional, social, and institutional conditions. It is obvious that this underemployed manpower has such strong ties — institutional (primarily insufficient collective child supervision), regional, and social (age, educational deprivation) in character — that a rise in aggregate demand does not seem to be a suitable method of solving the problem. For many of these groups outside the labor force, elasticity of supply is limited and a further vigorous expansion of selective labor market policy is needed.

Has Economic Balance Been Maintained during the Period?

If economic balance is defined as price stability, the answer is clearly negative. The demand inflation of the fifties has turned into the cost inflation of the sixties. But this is a trivial assertion which holds — with certain variations — for most Western European countries during substantial parts of the postwar period. Of greater interest is the question whether the increasingly ambitious goal of employment policy has obstructed stabilization efforts or whether the "new labor market policy" has contributed to a reduction in the conflict.

To give some indication of whether Swedish economic policy has been successful in mitigating the conflict between stability and full employment, we have calculated the Phillips relationship for Sweden. The Phillips curve (see Fig. 5-6) is based on observations regarding wage drift and unemployment for workers in the manufacturing industry during the period 1956-65. Although the range of variation in unemployment is small, correlation between wage drift and unemployment is very strong for this period ($r = -0.93$). If, on the other hand, calculations are made for the period 1956-70, the larger part of the correlation ($r = -0.42$) disappears. Observations for the years 1966-70 show increasing deviations from the curve. It is not possible to calculate the Phillips relationship for total wage increase and unemployment, since most wage agreements run for two or more years; a Phillips relationship calculated on the basis of yearly observations would lose its meaning. However, the addition of negotiated wage increase to wage drift does not change the overall picture.

It seems then that the Phillips curve has shifted to the right during the second half of the sixties, so that the steeper part of the curve occurs at a higher level of unemployment than it did previously. Also, it seems that this phenomenon can be explained by the fact that wage drift — that part of wage

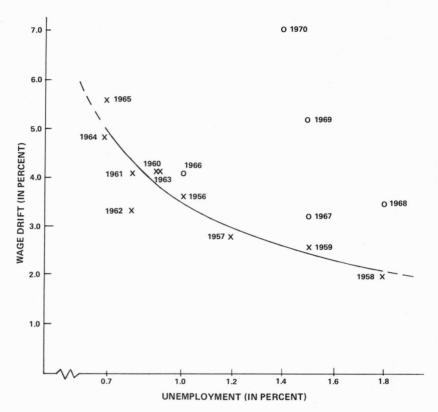

Figure 5-6. The Phillips Curve for Industrial Workers, 1956–1965
($r = -0.93$). Observations marked o are not included in the
calculations of the Phillips curve.

determination which occurs outside of central wage negotiations – has
changed.

In a study of the relationship between the situation on the labor market
and wage increases for workers in the manufacturing industry during the
period 1956–70, Assar Lindbeck has used the number of vacancies minus the
number of unemployed as a labor market variable (Fig. 5-7).[38] Observations
of this variable and of wage drift fit a linear relationship rather well. The
reason is that vacancies have increased more than employment.

Each observed rate of unemployment during the period 1966–70 is associated with a larger number of vacancies than was the same rate of unemployment during the previous period. In other words, the imbalance between

[38] Assar Lindbeck, "Is Stabilization Possible?" February 1971, mimeographed.

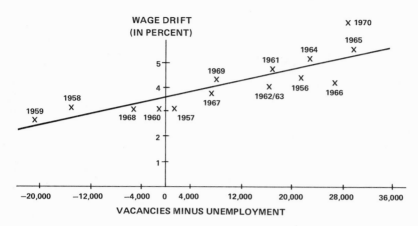

Figure 5-7. Interrelation between Labor Market Situation and Rate of Wage
Drift for Industrial Workers. X = coinciding observations for
two years. (From Assar Lindbeck, "Is Stabilization Possible?"
February 1971, mimeographed)

supply and demand in the labor market has grown worse. This has happened
in spite of the fact that the resources of labor market policy have almost
doubled. The greater part of these rapidly expanding resources has been
allocated to measures of adjustment — above all, to retraining and to location
policy measures.

It is difficult to give a clear explanation of this recent development. The
growing problems of employment policy may to a large extent be ascribed to
the accelerated rate of structural change which took place in the economy
during the sixties. Both internal and external factors have played a part in this
development. Because of reduced tariff barriers and transport costs, more and
more sectors of the economy have felt international competition. This in turn
underlies a markedly lower degree of self-financing in enterprises, as compared to the high level of the fifties. Concentration into larger units has
increased. Mergers of enterprises, followed by the closure of large parts of the
firms involved, have become frequent.[39] Several empirical studies of closings
in Sweden have shown that a considerable number of those dismissed remain
unemployed for a long period.

The statistical data about warnings of closures collected by the Labor
Market Board[40] show an increase of 200–300 percent in the number of
workers affected between the period 1960–65 and the period 1966–70. Fig-

[39] *Koncentrationsutredningen* [Concentration Study], SOU 1968:7 (Stockholm,
1968); Bengt Rydén, *Fusioner i svensk industri* [Mergers in Swedish Industry] (Stockholm, 1971), p. 208.

[40] See n. 43.

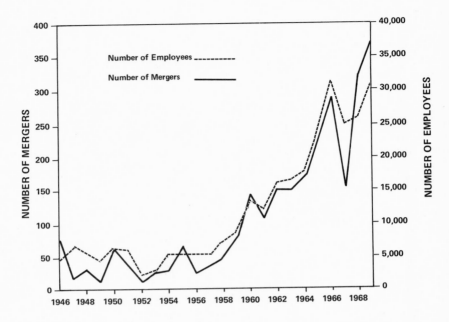

Figure 5-8. Number of Mergers and Number of Employees in Merged Firms,
1946–1969 (From Bengt Rydén, *Fusioner i svensk industri*
[Mergers in Swedish Industry][Stockholm, 1971], p. 208)

ures for the first quarter of 1971 show that the acceleration continues. The
task of employment policy was made harder by the concentration of structural change in certain industries and certain regions. The regional range of
variation from highest to lowest unemployment has increased. It is above all in
the so-called forest counties that unemployment has increased as compared to
the corresponding phase of the economic cycle during the previous period.
Long-term unemployment has grown ($\geq$ 13 weeks). This is true for both men
and women, but especially for men in the higher age groups. The somewhat
smaller increase for women can probably be explained by their greater mobility into and out of the labor force.

Thus employment policy has not succeeded in shifting the Phillips curve
toward *origo*. This failure is due mainly to the abovementioned problems.
Moreover, responsible politicans and authorities have never given labor market policy only the narrow objective of stabilization. The high priority given
to the full employment goal is based on social considerations also. Therefore,
it would be erroneous to judge all measures of labor market policy by their
stabilizing effects alone.

CONCLUSIONS AND RECOMMENDATIONS

The main question is whether the poor, or at any rate uneven, level of performance is caused by shortcomings of the model for economic policy or by a faulty or incomplete application of it. The impact of government policy on total demand — which here, in a simplified presentation, is supposed to reflect "general" measures — has, during the postwar period, shown less and less amplitude, while expenditures for selective manpower policy have risen vigorously (though jerkily — i.e., most vigorously during recessions). This, however, does not necessarily prove that Rehn's model has been applied wholeheartedly. The weakness of fiscal policy in Sweden may be related to smaller international cyclical fluctuations and to consequent weaker repercussions on Swedish exports and the Swedish economy as a whole. The smaller variations in the volume of exports toward the end of the period (see Table 5-4) indicate that such is the case. The scope for a vigorous anticyclical fiscal policy diminished during the sixties as the importance of balance of payments grew. A weak fiscal policy may also reflect lower stabilization ambitions; to that extent it would be a deliberate step. Finally, a milder fiscal policy can be interpreted, in accordance with government statements quoted previously, as an attempt to apply Rehn's model. Only a penetrating analysis beyond the scope of this paper will reveal which one of these possible explanations is correct or whether, as seems likely, all contributed to this development.

If, for the sake of argument, we regard economic policy as an attempt to apply Rehn's model, it is hard to avoid the impression that efforts have been half-hearted and asymmetrical. At the prospect of recession, traditional anticyclical policy was indeed abandoned, and selective manpower policy was expanded. But obviously the application of the model was less successful during booms, when much more restraint by general methods was called for. It has proved easier — politically — to use selective assistance as an alternative to general measures to maintain purchasing power during downswings than actively to subdue excess demand during booms and thereafter to "catch" detrimental employment effects by means of selective manpower policy. Moreover, general demand-maintaining measures taken during recessions have often been called off belatedly and thus have operated far into cyclical upswings. One of the main advantages of Rehn's model, a quick and effective way to meet the strains of a boom, has thereby been lost.

The nature of the problem mentioned, the absence of symmetry in the application of the model, is political, not technical. It is difficult and it takes considerable political courage systematically to force down the level of demand in a phase of expansion to the extent required by Rehn's model. In public opinion the employment goal is of prime importance. Restraint on expansion can in political debate be labeled as neglect of employment problems. The idea of sustained selective action during good years has not been realized. We must admit also that the application of the model has been hampered by a vigorous trend toward faster structural adjustment, faster rejection of disadvantaged groups, growing pressure from new groups previously left out of the labor force, and a manifest risk of educational and regional segregation in the labor market. At the same time, part of public opinion in Sweden has grown critical of a stabilization and growth model which, it is thought, neglects welfare components related to the process of adjustment required — e.g., the human costs of relocation.

Practical recommendations for modifying and extending Rehn's model can be summarized as follows:

1. A consistent anticyclical policy using fiscal policy as its main instrument is the prime prerequisite for successful stabilization efforts. Its aim should be preventive, not corrective, which calls for, on the one hand, a better forecasting technique and, on the other, a more flexible budget technique. The minister of finance should be granted the power to vary the rates of value-added taxation, vary the right to make tax-free deductions for investment purposes, and take other measures of a general nature (e.g., change the rules regarding allocations to investment reserve funds, advance or postpone changes in employers' dues already decided on in principle, etc.). Parliament, of course, should have the right to suspend such decisions, and to assume the political implications this may have for a government.

2. Selective measures, which at the present time are manifestly anticyclical, should be evened out over the cycle. The "stairway pattern" should be replaced by a smoothly rising curve. The corrective ("tidying up") function of manpower policy should be complemented by preventive functions such as intensified retraining activities, removal assistance, location away from areas of labor shortage, and strengthened support to the handicapped, older workers, women, etc. During booms a shift in emphasis from employment-creating to adjustment-promoting measures is called for.

3. Structural disparity in the evolution of a postindustrial society which is dependent on international developments is so significant that a steadily growing volume of selective measures is required. Rehn's model is basically a model for stability and growth, but structural factors obstruct the application of the model. Therefore, the total volume of necessary selective measures is continuously pushed to higher levels. Retraining, location, and removal aid are no longer sufficient to integrate less attractive manpower into the labor force, not even in situations of great excess demand, much less in terms of the equilibrium aimed at for stabilization purposes. The functions of manpower policy must be enlarged to include contributions to the creation of a more humane work environment and/or wage subsidies for submarginal manpower.

4. Further policy expansion should aim at integrating manpower policy with industrial policy relative to industrial structure. If the previous analysis is correct, a much greater share will be required for manpower policy than its present 1½ percent of the GNP. The shift of emphasis from short-term efforts limited in time and space to more extensive programs involving long-term action requires a clearer definition of the targets of industrial policy.

APPENDIX

The Effectiveness of Swedish Manpower Policy

A Brief Survey of a Number of Follow-up Studies

In relation to the scope of labor market policy in Sweden, the volume of cost-benefit research on the subject is still very limited. Not until 1967 did the minister of labor appoint a group of experts for cost-benefit studies in order to examine the macroeconomic impact of various labor market policy measures. The projects initiated so far are concerned with retraining (based on inquiries among 2,000 enrollees in four counties whose progress is followed for 2½ years), immigration (based on interviews with 4,000 immigrants and 1,000 Swedes), social processes in connection with geographic mobility, and information activities of the employment services. None of these has yet reached the point at which results can been published. The following survey covers a number of minor studies which had only limited ambitions.

Employment Services

For the twelve-month period May 1, 1966, to April 30, 1967, the Labor Market Board calculated the total number of job placements made and the share the employment services had in them.[41]

Total labor turnover for the period amounted to 1.5 million placements, or 46 percent of the number of persons employed at the end of the period. The role played by employment services rose sharply with the frequency of job change:

Number of placements per person	1	2	3	4
Percentage of placements made through employment services	21.9	29.5	52.6	57.3

The share of employment services in total labor turnover probably was from 20 to 25 percent and was mainly concentrated in manufacturing, the building

[41]G. Faragó, "Arbetskraftsomsättningen och de utnyttjade informationskällorna" [Labor Turnover and Sources of Information Used], 1967, mimeographed.

industry, and services. This estimate was confirmed by an inquiry among members of the LO (Confederation of Trade Unions) in 1968.[42] Of all those who had taken measures to change their occupation, 28.5 percent had visited the employment service; for those who wanted to change their place of work, the corresponding figure was 19.8 percent.

The role of employment services is especially important in connection with the closing of enterprises, the number of which has grown strongly during recent years as a consequence of an ever-increasing structural rationalization.[43] Closures are concentrated in a few industries (primarily textiles and clothing industries) and often affect localities with little diversification activity. Experience of these closings shows that employment services do have the resources to place an overwhelming majority of the unemployed, but that a residual unemployment on the order of from 10 to 15 percent ensues, affecting older workers, handicapped workers, women, and those who are least skilled. Residual unemployment often leads not to open unemployment but to early retirement, sheltered employment, or disappearance from the labor force.[44]

The study released most recently concerns the closing of forty-six enterprises having more than 5,000 employees during the period January 1968–March 1969.[45] From three to twelve months after closure, two-thirds of the workers had new jobs. Only 10 percent were unemployed in the formal sense; the remaining 15 percent participated in retraining, relief work, vocational rehabilitation, were ill, had retired, or left the labor force for other reasons.

In reality, the course of events after the closing of an enterprise is less propitious than the high proportion of replaced workers may lead one to believe. For one thing, a considerable number of those replaced have to accept lower wages and/or less advantageous conditions in their new places of work.[46] For another, the official purpose of employment service activities ("employment services shall aim at helping the dismissed to an employment

---

[42] Lars Nyrén, "Omställningar och anpassningsproblem på arbetsplatsen" [Adjustment and Adjustment Problems on the Job] (Stockholm, 1969), mimeographed.

[43] Since the mid-fifties, data have been available about advance warning of dismissals by firms having ten or more employees. The number of employees affected by the warning of a cutdown in production and of plant shutdowns has been as follows: 1960, 6,730; 1961, 8,270; 1962, 9,990; 1963, 8,110; 1964, 4,310; 1965, 8,890; 1966, 20,730; 1967, 24,500; 1968, 22,670; 1969, 10,920; 1970, 20,960; 1971, 37,000.

[44] A number of studies about closures are reported in R. Meidner, "The Employment Problems of Individuals and Groups," paper presented at the International Conference on Automation, Full Employment, and a Balanced Economy, Rome, 1967.

[45] "Report regarding Measures in Connection with the Closure during the Period January 1968–March 1969 of Forty-six Enterprises," September 1969, mimeographed.

[46] Lars Nyrén, "Omställningar."

equivalent to or better than the one they leave," in which process persons involved shall be given the opportunity to make "a free and considerate choice of work") cannot be realized, in spite of the intensive and active operation of employment services.[47]

Retraining

The Labor Market Board has made a series of follow-up studies regarding the employment effect of retraining. Such inquiries were made about trainees, whose retraining was terminated in the late fifties and the early sixties. The results are shown in Table 5-10. Taking into consideration the fact that the participants had been unemployed or hard to place, the outcome seems to have been a success. The proportion of placements was high in the case of all inquiries, independently of the duration of the observation period, which would indicate that it was possible to integrate trainees into work life in a lasting manner. Labor market training has also made employment prospects much better for especially hard to place workers, such as handicapped and older persons. Applicants for vocational rehabilitation who have received labor market training (1964), also have been the object of follow-up studies. Of 3,000 male enrollees, almost 80 percent got jobs three months after completion of the course; of about 1,000 women, a good 70 percent became employed. Employment services accounted for 76 percent of placements, of which 90 percent were for work in the open market. From 20 to 25 percent had to abandon gainful employment during the three-year period of observation. The rehabilitation effect of retraining was least effective in the case of the socially maladjusted (former prisoners and alcoholics) and the mentally defective. The fact that more than half the total group was still gainfully employed three years after training (83 percent of them for contractual wages) points to a considerable macroeconomic (socioeconomic) net effect of educational input.

A somewhat more sophisticated, though very limited study of the effects of retraining has been carried out on 500 persons who in 1965 had gone through labor market courses of at least 20 weeks' duration in the northern county of Västerbotten.[48] 76% of the trainees obtained employment in the intended occupation and wages that exceeded the income to be expected

[47]William Peterson, "Vad kostar en företagsnedläggning den drabbade arbetskraften?" [What are the Costs of a Closure for the Workers Involved?], in *Arbetslivet i kris och förvandling* [Work Life in Crisis and Change], ed. Casten v. Otter (Stockholm, 1971).

[48]Åke Dahlberg, "Funktionell rörlighetsstimulans på arbetsmarknaden i Västerbottens län" [Mobility Stimuli in the Labor Market of Västerbotten], Umeå, 1968, mimeographed, as summarized in Gösta Rehn, *Economic Implications of Training Programmes* (Paris: OECD, 1969).

Table 5-10. Employment Status for Labor Market Trainees
after Training

(percentages)

Employment Status	1st Quarter of 1959[a]	Period of Training			
		All of 1960[b]		March-April 1963[c]	
		Male	Female	Male	Female
Total Employed	75	77	70	88	81
in occupation for which trained	54	–	–	–	–
in closely related occupation	11	–	–	–	–
in other occupation	10	–	–	–	–
Seeking Work	16	3	3	2	3
Not in Labor Force	9	20	27	10	16
Total	100	100	100	100	100

Source: Sweden, Labor Market Board.

[a]Three months after the end of training.
[b]About two years after the end of training.
[c]About one year after the end of training.

without training by about one-third. The cumulative value of expected net income during a period of ten years, discounted to present value, was calculated to be 10,000–12,000 kr. for the average trainee, whose training costs amounted to 3,000 kr. Thus the benefit-cost ratio would be from 3 to 4, and the payoff period about twenty-five months. The macroeconomic cost-benefit calculation, however, is subject to greater uncertainty. Given certain assumptions about the rate of discount and the multiplier effect of employment created by retraining, the capitalized value of expected returns for the economy as a whole is estimated to result in a benefit-cost ratio of about 5 and a payoff period of some twenty months. Thus the calculation ascribes to retraining substantial benefits both for the individual and for the economy as a whole.

Removal

In the early sixties the Labor Market Board made a number of studies about persons who had received so-called starting allowances in connection with removal; most were younger men without vocational education.

At the end of the period of observation (from one to two years) only 3 percent were jobless, but more than half had left their first place of employment and almost half had moved back to their home county. From these studies the general conclusion can be drawn that, for many people, removal assistance does not lead to permanent relocation but primarily serves to help unemployed young persons to get a job.

A sociological study of the adjustment of workers who moved to Gothenburg in the fall of 1966[49] — both those who obtained removal assistance and others — showed that 25–30 percent had moved away after seven months. Among the reasons stated for moving away from Gothenburg, dissatisfaction with housing and with the work situation predominated. The migrants had as high a rate of unemployment after their return as before moving to Gothenburg. The fact that the result of the inquiry in this respect is markedly less favorable than that of the study of assisted migrants (i.e., those who obtained starting allowances) referred to previously may be explained in part by the fact that the Gothenburg inquiry was carried out during a period of slack employment.

Sheltered Employment

An inquiry into the profitability of a dozen sheltered workshops with 530 employees was made for the period 1963–65.[50] Net effect was defined as

$$R_t - C_t - W_t - K_t,$$

where

R_t = sales value of goods and services produced during period t;

C_t = cost of raw material, semifinished products, other material, and external services;

W_t = value of income from alternative activities forfeited by able-bodied persons employed in the workshop during period t; and

K_t = capital cost during period t.

The analysis revealed a net profit in almost 50 percent of the workshops and moderate losses (not exceeding 3,000 kr. per employee) in the others. If one could allow for the rehabilitation effect and the positive effect on relatives' earned incomes (no longer reduced), the net effect would be markedly greater. It seems natural to conclude that sheltered workshops, which nor-

[49] Bengt G. Rundblad, "Inflyttad arbetskrafts anpassning i en expanderande arbetsmarknad" [Adjustment of Migrant Workers in an Expanding Labor Market], in *Arbetslivet*, ed. Casten v. Otter.

[50] *Arbetsmarknadsverket och arbetsmarknadspolitiken* [The Labor Market Administration and Labor Market Policy] (Stockholm, 1969).

mally show financial losses, are justifiable from a macroeconomic point of view. To this should be added their indisputable noneconomic value.

Location Policy

Since the foremost objective of location policy is to support employment, its effect should be measured by the number of new employment opportunities created, as compared to a hypothetical development in the absence of location policy measures. During the period July 1, 1965–December 31, 1970, 1,363,000,000 kr. were granted in locating loans and contributions to 651 enterprises.[51] Total investment costs for these projects amounted to 2,607,000,000 kr. In their applications, the firms had indicated a planned increase in employment of 18,584 jobs, but the actual increase was only 12,932 by the turn of the year 1970/71. The deficit was due in part to the fact that time had been too short to execute the plans. See Table 5-11.

Table 5-11. Planned and Actual Increase in Employment in
Assisted Enterprises, 1965–1970

Assistance Granted in	Number of Enterprises Supported	Planned Increases in Employment	Actual Increase in Employment	Actual Increase as % of Planned Increase
1965	90	3,491	2,887	83
1966	114	5,212	3,088	59
1967	63	2,541	2,228	88
1968	88	1,708	1,787	105
1969	111	3,120	2,570	82
1970	118	2,512	369	15
Total 584		18,584	12,929 Average	70

Source: *Regionalekonomiska meddelanden* [Regional Economic Information], 1970, p. 1.

Trend calculations indicate that the increase in employment in support areas has resulted to a significant extent from public development assistance. However, this has been obtained at the substantial cost of, on the average, 105,000 kr. in public grants for each new employment opportunity. If all costs are included, the total figure amounts to almost 200,000 kr. (400,000 kr. in the northernmost county). Only detailed and complicated calculations will show whether costs on this order of magnitude yield a net return for the economy as a whole. Comparison should be made with the costs for alternative solutions. The Ministry of Labor and Housing has appointed a research group to initiate a project in this area.

[51] *Regionalekonomiska meddelanden* [Regional Economic Information], 1970, no. 1.

INDEX

Age: as barrier to mobility, 20; and dispersion of unemployment rates, 16, 29-31; and labor force composition, 44-46; and participation rates, 141-43; and qualifications for new jobs, 48n; in segmentation of labor force, 27
Aid to Families with Dependent Children, growth of, 109
Antidiscrimination policy, 12
Antidiscrimination programs, 88, 89
Aukrust, O., on Swedish economy, 119
Automation, national concern about, 99

Banfield, Edward C., on time preference, 92
Benefit-cost study: of manpower programs, 11-12, 90, 91; of Sweden's manpower policy, 153, 156
Blacks: and "credentialism," 4; incomes of, 85-86, 87, 89, 101; job turnover rates of, 19, 26; and job vacancies, 27; and manpower policy, 115-16; mobility of, 20; in poverty, 85; projected share of, in labor force, 47; time preference of, 92-93; unemployment rates of, 31-32, 79-80, 87
Blue-collar occupations: in Sweden, 122-23; women in, 35

Child care: funds for, 81, 106; need for, 80-81; provided by government, 109-10

Children. See Child care
Civil rights legislation: as manpower policy, 27; and racial dispersion of unemployment, 31-32
Clerical occupations: nonwhites in, 32; women in, 36
Cohen, Malcolm, on manpower program enrollments, 40-41
Collective bargaining: and shift to younger labor force, 46; as source of labor market imperfections, 7
College Work-Study program, enrollment in, 41
Color. See Nonwhites; Race
Compartmentalization: of labor market, 60, 68-74; terms of, 69. See also Segmentation
Computer system, of employment, 79, 81
Construction industry: frictional unemployment in, 19-20; mobility in, 19-20; seasonal unemployment in, 25-26
Cost-benefit ratio. See Benefit-cost study
Cost-push influences, and policy choices, 13
Council of Economic Advisers: on labor market, 76; and manpower policy, 13
Craftsmen and foremen occupations: nonwhites in, 32; unemployment rate of, 77; women in, 35
Creaming, as policy for manpower training programs, 90, 91-92, 93

159

Library of Congress Cataloging in Publication Data

Ulman, Lloyd.
    Manpower programs in the policy mix.

    Includes bibliographical references.
    1. Manpower policy – United States. I. Title.
HD5724.U55   331.1'1'0973   72–11850
ISBN 0–8018–1452–9

THE JOHNS HOPKINS UNIVERSITY PRESS

This book was composed in Press Roman text and Univers Bold display type by
Jones Composition Company, Inc. from a design by Edward Scott. It was printed
by Universal Lithographers, Inc., on Warren's 60-lb. Sebago, regular finish, and
bound by L. H. Jenkins, Inc., in Columbia Bayside linen.

DATE DUE